# DESIGN AND LANDSCAPE FOR PEOPLE

This book is dedicated to our children

Finbar Kelly

Eve, Thea, Merle & Rita Rogers

# DESIGN AND LANDSCAPE FOR PEOPLE

## NEW APPROACHES TO RENEWAL

Clare Cumberlidge and Lucy Musgrave

With 269 color illustrations

Thames & Hudson

Locations of projects around the world. See contents opposite for project names.

First published in 2007 in hardcover in the United States of America by Thames & Hudson Inc., 500 Fifth Avenue, New York, New York 10110

thamesandhudsonusa.com

Library of Congress Catalog Card Number 2006908834

ISBN 978-0-500-34233-6

Printed and bound in China by Everbest Printing Co. Ltd

# Contents

# PREFACE Ralph Rugoff

This book is an essential resource for anyone interested in the changing social landscape of the twenty-first century. It brings together groundbreaking case studies from around the globe that track new developments in urban, suburban and rural renewal. Surveying projects and practices that trespass over the related fields of architecture, urban design, community development, landscape architecture and art, it charts an emerging geography of repair and regeneration that engages (often simultaneously) physical, social and economic scenarios. And in mapping a variety of approaches for re-deploying underutilized resources in teeming cities as well as in depopulated exurban areas, this book presents us with a set of evolving tools that can transform the way we perceive, conceive of, and initiate changes in, the places where we live.

In putting this survey together, Clare Cumberlidge and Lucy Musgrave have focused on interdisciplinary methods for renewal that emphasize citizen involvement. Whether they concentrate on re-branding local identities or on activities that re-knit social fabrics while revitalizing economic life, these approaches are designed to support long-term, sustainable development. They may be implemented by, or in collaboration with, grassroots organizations, artist-run collectives, NGOs or government agencies, yet critical to all of them is that they evolve strategies for change from the ground up.

In this very important respect the work documented in these pages stands apart from the top-down planning that characterized the twentieth century's culture of expertise. In contrast, the diverse practitioners described here – including architects, urbanists, artists and activitists – seek to break down boundaries between professional and amateur, expert and citizen. Rather than targeting singular objectives, their work focuses on processes that produce multiple benefits. So that, say, a campaign to build new homes for the urban poor results in the acquisition of new skills by local residents, enabling them to take on increased responsibility for future neighbourhood planning while altering their perceptions about their ability to engineer significant change in their environment. In other words, these practices aim to develop new subjectivities and attitudes as well as physical platforms for community development.

In conceptual terms, the growth of this emerging field reflects an urgent desire to build bridges between the disconnected worlds of planning, commerce, culture, technology and politics. Having learned from the disasters of modernist planning that the road to hell can be paved with good intentions, adherents of the new approach eschew any attempts to impose an idealized rationalism. Instead, they search for possible solutions by exploring the ground beneath the middle of local conflicts, tracing out an ad hoc logic that connects the disparate perspectives and needs of the communities they work with. The unruly 'subject' that modernist utopias seemed bent on disposing of is here reframed as the indispensable engine of long-term development – and as a crucial counterforce to the cycles of regional devastation and obsolescence produced by global capital's shifting flows and alliances.

The pioneering practitioners discussed in this book share an understanding that our present moment demands creative engagement and concrete proposals, rather than gestures of protest. But in undertaking practical projects they are also concerned with opening up new avenues of knowledge. And for anyone with the willingness to pay attention, exposure to this kind of work can be transformative. It helps us to imagine different possibilities for human society, even as it challenges us to understand better our societies as they exist today. Finally, the challenges addressed by these projects – in particular, the problem of redeveloping derelict and deprived communities – will only become more important in the years ahead, given the destabilizing effects of globalism. This book can serve as a beacon illuminating this crucial territory, while reminding us that our responsibility begins with the power to imagine.

# INTRODUCTION

This book seeks to define for the first time a radical emerging field of practice in urban and rural renewal that responds to the changing social landscape of the twenty-first century. While it can be seen as a source book or manual for policy-makers, planners and practitioners, it is also hoped that it will find a broader audience among all those concerned for the future of our habitats. Either way, it aims to inspire creative and effective responses to contexts of change. The projects featured are varied in scale and type and have very different results and outputs, but all were selected on the basis of the transferable strategies within them. They share common principles that are critical to their success: they are cross-disciplinary, socially engaged, environmentally aware and inventive. They offer new methodologies and new perspectives, demonstrating effective and pragmatic ways to tackle problems where current modes of operation often fail to produce genuine and lasting results.

Our subject, then, is the process of change in the built environment. A state of flux exists in urban centres and rural landscapes where cities shrink, new cities explode, issues of culture and identity are at the foreground and the traditional paradigms of development, governance and planning struggle to find ways to respond. In a global context, issues of urbanization, sustainability and planning have never been more pressing. This book presents a shift in practice which emerges from and responds to this context of flux, focusing specifically on the built environment as the vessel or catalyst for social, economic and ecological change.

The projects showcased in this book demonstrate a compelling apparatus with which to address difficult issues of ownership, use, perception and planning. They often tackle urban and rural environments that have lost their economic and/or social impetus. Some are sites that have been discounted, forgotten, or are peripheral, but the responses are energetic, surprising and playful. They cover issues of identity and characterization; social and physical infrastructure; carving out space – conceptual and physical – for public debate; revitalizing spaces for social interaction and play; participative design processes; and new economic structures.

The projects featured generally date from 1990 onwards and encompass everything from small temporary interventions to the planning of whole towns and regions. The works resist the narrow confines of the commonplace discourses on architecture, art and city planning. To describe or criticize the projects within the critical language and values of their discipline can escape the primary intention and the subtleties of approach which the projects make manifest. This introductory essay attempts to present a possible critical framework and a toolkit for practice which reflects the qualities and principles of this new field.

Playpump in South Africa uses the energy of children to provide unlimited clean water – a radical design solution to a longstanding social problem.

The Works Swimming Pool in Zollverein, Germany, is a public pool built by artists Dirk Paschke and Daniel Milohnic within the UNESCO World Heritage Site of a redundant colliery. The site is being transformed by a masterplan that is attempting to seed a new cultural economy.

How should governmental, non-governmental and commercial agents programme the renewal of deprived areas? This book is a marker within a live debate: a map of a new field and a challenge to existing practice. These are not marginal projects – they have a real relevance in tackling major contemporary problems and can produce results that far exceed the outputs of conventional regeneration practice.

## Global context

Sustainable development is one of the biggest challenges facing the world in the twenty-first century. The speed of population growth and urbanization sets social, political, cultural and environmental trends, not only making the management of urban settlements of critical importance but also with huge implications for land use and rural development. Governments and non-governmental agencies are struggling to define and manage these processes on a continental and localized scale. The United Nations Millennium Declaration – a commitment to improve the lives of 100 million slum dwellers by the year 2020 (a task mandated to UN-HABITAT) – becomes an almost token proposition when countered with the fact that by 2020 there will be at least 1.5 billion slum dwellers worldwide, of which 100 million is under seven per cent.

The terms used to describe this field are themselves limiting. Regeneration is the most current term used in the West to describe a process of addressing decline within deprived communities and specifically the post-industrial urban decline that is being experienced all over the western hemisphere. Over the last quarter-century strategy after strategy has been initiated to try to lift these areas and their communities out of poverty, lack of hope and lack of opportunity – to remediate a scarred physical landscape and encourage new economies to take root.

Renewal, in the USA at least, has become a problematic word in some quarters, associated with aggressive racial programmes under the guise of 'slum clearance' and particularly linked with the rebuilding of urban downtown areas that experienced 'white flight' and major economic decline in the 1960s and 1970s. Today it retains uncomfortable political overtones and a fluid meaning, associated with the New Urbanist movement as well as community-based grassroots initiatives.

In developing nations, the words 'regeneration' or 'renewal' are replaced with 'development' and 'upgrading'. These refer variously to the management of the process of mass urbanization (with the associated social upheaval, strain on infrastructure and ecological impact), and to the 'mainstreaming' of informal and uncontrolled, yet permanent,

The CLEAN-India programme trains children to monitor their environment, making them the knowledge base for their communities as well as campaigning at governmental level for change (see pp. 82–7).

settlements (slums, townships, refugee camps) into places that are ordered, controlled and normalized, whether by massive slum clearances or through the upgrading and rebuilding of the physical infrastructure.

And finally, over the last fifteen years there has emerged an increasing emphasis on 'sustainability': in the UK and US, in particular, 'sustainable communities' has become a key phrase in public policy. What sustainability, as a term, actually means is much debated, and it does not serve to enter into that debate here. Nevertheless, there may be seen to be a point at which 'help' (in the form of outside NGOs) is no longer needed – when, one might say, sustainability has been reached. At this point the community becomes self-sufficient enough, the economy strong and balanced enough, and the local ecology stable enough, to start self-renewing organically. This book showcases important and radical projects that demonstrate ways to reach this point, making communities more sustainable, exciting, inclusive and rooted places to live.

In considering how to tackle these problems, this new field of practice recognizes the need for utopian single visions to be replaced by multiple visions, frameworks where differing meanings and cultures can coexist. Adaptive transformations, which **use, reuse and shift existing infrastructures**, become more appropriate forms of vision – visions building on and working with existing contexts and meanings and cultures.

The destruction of local identity is perceived as a key threat from globalization. The approaches within this book embrace local specificity of response: key principles that run through all these projects are to embed the **participation of local people** and to **respect local distinctiveness** and character of culture and environment. However, placing projects from across the globe side by side demonstrates that common approaches based on simple principles can be applicable across scales and across continents. There are shared challenges – a lack of community cohesion, local pride, sustainable economy, a humane built environment and ecological respect are as evident in a small town in the rural USA as they are in Delhi or Johannesburg. The picture is a complex one: every 'developed country' contains a 'third world' of child poverty, malnutrition, unemployment, communicable diseases and inadequate housing. Similarly, every 'developing nation' has its 'first world' of immense wealth, globalized business, finance, fashion and technology. This book demonstrates that distinctions between 'first world' and 'third world' solutions are based on a false sense of differentiation. Third world areas deserve, if they are to become globally viable, the same level of physical infrastructure and sophisticated thinking as 'failing' areas of developed nations, who in return have much to learn from the techniques and processes being used in areas of few material resources but great reserves of creativity.

## A new field of practice?

We have established the need for creative and imaginative responses to global challenges of renewal, going beyond the existing terminologies. Our proposition here is that there is an emerging shared approach to these challenges across disciplines and sectors. Some of the projects in this book may be familiar to readers. Landschaftspark Duisburg Nord, for example, is a recognized exemplar within landscape architecture; De Strip a beacon of socially engaged artistic practice. However, the familiarity of the projects tends to be

The Kunstprojekte Riem allowed the growing community of a new suburb of Munich, Germany, to engage with the ongoing development process by expressing their feelings about the development, and building up new social networks in response.

confined to a particular sector and so the points of crossover of strategy or principle do not become clear. It is within this area of crossover that we believe the new field resides.

What are these shared principles? There is an awareness of the process of **renewal as being continuous**. This may seem obvious, but is not reflected in usual government or NGO fixed-term programmes. The approaches shown in our case studies make a crucial shift away from the idea of renewal as having a concrete aim and endpoint, and towards the idea of targeted interventions in a continuous process of change. This does not mean that nothing is ever 'achieved', since these projects demonstrate massive change by any measure of output: economic revival, social cohesion, environmental and ecological repair, shifts in perception, identity and pride. The difference is in the way that the projects approach their sites and their issues. Rather than a direct, causal approach to problems and their solutions, all these projects take a holistic, multidimensional approach to their designated situation, acknowledging the heterogeneity of places and their communities. The understanding of change as continuous means that practice must acknowledge the importance of long-term thinking and the need to create space for ongoing development and adaptation.

It might seem that much of the work we are considering has taken place in **contexts of poverty** and with minimal resources. Does that mean that poverty truly is the mother of invention and if so, what are the implications of this? To advocate poverty as a stimulus

The Rural Studio in Alabama, USA, works in a context of minimal resources and creatively uses educational structures to create physical change. Pictured here is the new multifunctional building in Newbern, which serves as a fire station and a town hall (see pp. 126–36).

to creativity would be an uncomfortable conclusion and, in fact, many of these projects also take place in contexts of wealth. What all the projects share is a commitment towards **maximization of resources** – material, human or economic – and a strategic approach towards achieving maximum effect with minimal means. There are other factors which also produce these elegant and creative approaches to societal challenges. It seems that pressure on resources results in inventiveness of response, a clear understanding of objective, and an appreciation of the value of reuse or adaptation of existing built or social infrastructures. Bureaucracy does not stifle but is incorporated as one of the tools for change. There is a new openness to the value of partnership and **collaboration** within and between practitioners, community groups, agencies, and private and public sector organizations.

This shifting field is also marked by an awareness of **symbolic value, the understanding of the significance of meaning within place.** This understanding underpins three different aspects of our new field: the belief in the effectiveness of the small action; the use of local distinctiveness and values as starting points within visions for the future; and the emergence of integrated programmes of identity within planning and implementation.

Perhaps one of the most significant shifts we have identified within this new field is that of the **professional operating outside their normal sphere of practice**. Artists are devising civic maintenance programmes, engineers are developing programmes of social and educational advocacy, a theatre group is running a children's town. The range of practitioners involved is broad, including engineers, artists, planners, architects and environmentalists. In nearly every case study in this book the individual practitioner has moved outside and beyond his or her own discipline to work in a broader, more strategic and critical role. This may be allied to a renewed recognition that 'regeneration' or 'renewal' is not merely a task for city planners, economists, architects or politicians.

An example of how an artist can act as a catalyser within wider processes of development, both physical and social, is Kerstin Bergendal's work at the new suburb of Trekroner in Denmark. There she instigated a series of workshops for a variety of practitioners, users and decision-makers, requesting that they leave their professional status at the door on arrival, thereby freeing up a discussion of principles rather than a series of assumptions about professional territorial positions. The many outputs of this work included built projects in the new terrain. One, a bridge, the first physical infrastructure built by the artist Nils Norman, demonstrates the strategic ways many – perhaps all – disciplines can and do contribute to processes of urban and rural development in often unexpected ways if given the physical and intellectual space to contribute. The motivation across the board is a desire to effect change

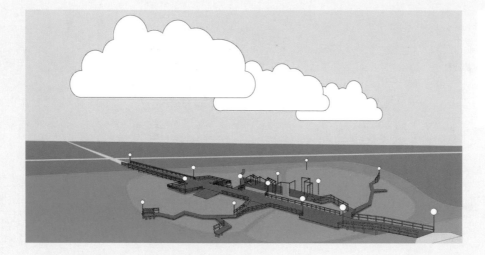

The artist Nils Norman's design for a new bridge in Trekroner, Denmark, developed with support from the landscape architect Ib Asger Olsen. The bridge functions as a playful multifunctional public space as well as a literal and metaphorical bridge between the inhabitants of the new town of Trekroner and the University of Roskilde opposite.

in the most targeted possible way, combining the expertise of professionals with the fresh perspectives that can come from stepping outside of narrow professional definitions and their territories.

### Participation

We are currently undergoing a massive shift towards participative culture. This is evident globally in terms of policy and governance and shifts in corporate practice, professional practice, the media, and the digital revolution. Global trends in participative processes have developed fast since Agenda 21, the UN's 1992 statement on sustainable development, which put the community at the heart of local decision-making through its widespread adoption by local governments. But it is not only local governance: the widespread adoption of consumer-input to product development, a television culture that no longer sees audiences as passive, a new open source approach towards the development of ideas and processes, means that we are moving towards a new model of network over the previously dominant model of hierarchy.

In the 1990s many practitioners and organizations developed pioneering models and strategies to unsettle conventional hierarchies between user and producer. These ranged from participative city governance to campaigning environmental and cultural organizations to individual creative practitioners who challenged the institutional norms.

What became clear during this period was the critical value of an independent catalyst or facilitating organization which could initiate a public debate about the changes in civic society and which could bring the tools to enable different communities and stakeholders to participate within this debate. A number of projects, like many staged by Common Ground (see pp. 168–71) or the Architecture Foundation in London, have tested ways of radically broadening the client group, challenging the assumption that one key decision-maker is responsible as the client. Through these projects the specificity of local understanding and knowledge has been used to radically inform the development and quality of a brief, and therefore to ensure that the response has a greater chance of long-term success. The practice of framing key questions for a wide and inclusive debate about the implications of change is one that has grown exponentially over the past twenty years.

Challenging the 'tick box' approach to community consultation, advocating the democratization of decision-making, and testing methods of widening the client group were strategies of participation that were explored throughout the 1990s. New methods of engagement were established that often focused on asking difficult questions and/or capturing the input of marginalized communities in areas of deprivation and areas of massive physical change. Not only did activists challenge the notion of who makes decisions for whom, but also who has the right to participate. Previously overlooked citizens from the housebound to the newly arrived refugee were now seen as critical participants. What many of these strategies shared was the principle of putting information clearly in the public domain and drawing together a debate between a public, political and professional audience to unlock different perspectives and produce different solutions. Dissemination of tools and the development of new planning processes became the outputs.

In the fundamental shift towards a participative and network model, which we are now experiencing, hierarchies will be further broken down. Working in an environment of complexity and flux, the intermediary becomes more necessary and more important. While satisfaction of users/residents can be a laudable goal within regenerative schemes, there is also a need to aspire to much more than this. Civic space cannot be static, but must be able to accommodate conflict, friction, debate, difference and multiplicity. The role of artists in framing and inserting key questions into planning and development processes, and in creating space for dissention and debate, has been of particular interest in the last ten years.

Artists have identified an increasing opportunity to work with social and institutional dynamics as their material. They have carved out the physical and conceptual space under the noses of the conventional powers – creating their own space for this work and intervening within debates and decision-making processes. The Austrian group WochenKlausur have pioneered the field of art as social intervention, employing a rigorous methodology utilizing their privileged position as artists in developing concrete proposals in response to local socio-political problems. Translating their proposals into action, their aim is to produce small but effective improvements.

The artist Jeanne van Heeswijk's current project, the Blue House, is developing a new model of artist's intervention within planning and community-building processes. The Blue House is a new dwelling which the artist has secured in the large-scale in-progress housing development on the reclaimed island of Ijberg in Amsterdam. The Blue House is a 'housing association for the mind': it hosts residencies, short and long term, for film-makers, philosophers, horticulturalists, artists, curators, architects, all of whom research or produce work relating to the formation of new communities. The project also offers sensitive and pragmatic interventions to assist Ijberg's new community, such as the development of a vegetable garden offering free fresh vegetables to residents who would otherwise have to travel thirty minutes to the nearest greengrocer. This is seen as an integral part of a critical response to current planning processes. The significance of the Blue House lies in its commitment to become part of the processes of development on a long-term basis and its ability to operate outside of any particular agency's patronage; the Blue House itself becomes an **active and independent agent of change**.

As more and more practitioners adopt these strategic and specific investigations into planning, housing, infrastructure, societal change and participation, new network models are forming. They rely on rigorous methodologies, low-cost tools, sophisticated communication and dissemination strategies, and radical thinking.

## Openness

A second key theme within these case studies, arising from the recognition of regeneration as a continuous process of change, has been **the idea of the unfinished**. Most new developments – from the Disney town of Celebration in the USA or the Prince Charles-sponsored Poundbury development in Dorset, to new suburbs in London or new cities in China – are complete settlements planned around more or less generally understood principles of urban design with varying degrees of consideration for provision of social spaces and amenities. Both when 'successful' in 'place-making' (streetscape, active frontages, mix of uses) and when deemed 'unsuccessful' (ambiguous, semi-private corporate sphere, inhuman scale; car-dominance, i.e. prioritizing parking over pedestrian flow; no active frontages etc.), these developments are strangely discomforting. This discomfort comes out of the lack of authenticity but also crucially out of the very 'finishedness' of the

The Blue House is a villa originally intended for private sale, in the centre of the first wave of development on Ijberg, an island in Amsterdam's docklands. The Blue House provides the only community space on the island where new residents can meet, as well as housing a living, reflective record of the development of the area, through its residencies and projects.

new quarters. There is no **space left for appropriation** by the community. The community cannot grow through adaptive inhabitation of the town; and if changes in the wider context threaten the predetermined vision of the future embedded within the design, there are no ways that the spaces (physical and social) can adapt in response.

It seems that a prerequisite for success understood by this new practice is that planning and architecture must leave space open for opportunity. This openness should allow for both irrationality in the process and community appropriation of the spaces as development takes place. Temporary and longer time-limited programmes have an important role to play in this, such as the case studies of De Strip (see pp. 100–105) in a European context, and the Slum Networking project in India (see pp. 62–7), where providing the highest quality of infrastructure in a highly participative but financially economic way creates the space for residents to build for themselves. New suburbs in Northern Europe are beginning to tackle this issue, developing processes of planning new settlements which allow space for change and adaptation. Creative programmes addressing appropriation and openness during planning and early build of new suburbs have been tested in Messestadt Riem, Germany, and Trekroner, Denmark (see pp. 73 and 148).

Process is a key term in considering points of shared principle in this new field. Objects, buildings and designs may result from these exemplary projects but principally they are the conduit for processes of social change and not the primary objective. Artists and other practitioners are acting to frame and conceptualize a process rather than to produce works of art, architecture or engineering. This raises interesting **questions around critical assessment** of these projects. If the building is secondary, how do we judge the architecture? If the artwork is immaterial, how do we understand its value? In fact there is a rigour of approach, a conceptual underpinning which can serve to communicate, understand and evaluate the projects. This rigorous conceptual framework does not deny aesthetic value; indeed, the integrity of the process translates into integrity of material response. Within architecture, this new ethical approach demands a design response that embraces environmental sustainability, longevity and weathering, and a quality of detailing and materiality that is appropriate to the long-term or short-term purpose of the structure rather than the generic twenty-year lifespan assumed of most contemporary construction.

## Conclusions

The field of practice that we are beginning to frame here is both new and rooted in the philosophical and practical debates of many preceding decades. There are clear conceptual

A street in Ahmedabad, India, transformed by the innovations of the Slum Networking approach (pp. 62–7) to infrastructural design.

links both to early propositions from radical community planning and experimental social architecture of the 1960s and 1970s in the USA and UK, and to artistic practice and the environmental movement growing from the 1980s. However, in the last fifteen years a new generation has reached maturity and is beginning to shift into wider recognition, in turn spawning a further generation of practitioners and thinkers whose base in action research is producing important results. This book showcases both representatives of the older generation that is now mainstreaming – Slum Networking, Common Ground, Landschaftspark Duisburg Nord – and lesser-known but groundbreaking projects such as Hotel Neustadt or the Nelson Mandela Museum. These projects have been initiated by communities themselves, activists or practitioners (artists, architects, engineers) as much as by conventional clients (government agencies, commercial developers) but demonstrate easily replicable processes and approaches that can be applied to many different sites.

The field is evolving and continually shifting. Regeneration and renewal projects worldwide can learn from these approaches, bringing this international best practice to bear on how current and future development is tackled. Clients (whether governmental, agency or private sector), practitioners and citizens are increasingly seeking effective ways of producing change. We believe these case studies offer real insight into how to collaborate, absorbing the central principles about continuous change, participation, interdisciplinary working and the importance of local identity. Ethics and ways of working that avoid the traditional (reductive and narrow) view of 'rules' and 'guidelines', but that, rather, celebrate quality and integrity, will provide greater strategic bearing and long-term efficacy for the capital and revenue investments as well as the sheer energy and ingenuity of human creativity and collaboration.

The Koliagbe Poultry Farm in Guinea created a new approach to improving the country's nutrition through education, alongside architectural innovation in use of materials and design. Its innovation is to combine and 'layer' programmes of healthcare, education and the rural economy, centred around an improvement in diet through breeding chickens. The project resulted from an extraordinary collaboration between Alpha Diallo, a Guinean agronomist, his uncle Bachis Diallo, a veterinarian, Ella Kivekäs, a Finn and the patron of the project, and Heikkinen-Komonea, Finnish architects.

Infrastructure is the essential framework of every community. As such it can be defined in many ways: the hard infrastructure of roads, railways, communications systems, water, sewers and power lines; the social infrastructure of schools, post offices, hospitals and social services; and the environmental infrastructure of green spaces and waterways. The metaphor of a city as a body, with the infrastructure as the bones, blood vessels, lungs and intestines, is much repeated and not inappropriate. The utility of our urban infrastructure relies on both the physical provision and the systems of planning and maintenance – a broad consideration of services and supply.

The provision of infrastructure, its maintenance and upgrading is conventionally viewed as a problem for engineers that requires a fixed 'best value' solution derived from rational calculation and linear processes that draw on accepted norms. Fast-paced change has meant the desertion of obsolete infrastructure rather than its adaptation or reuse. Replacement too often results in new structures that cut through the surrounding urban fabric or landscape with no regard for particularities of place, severing communities and entailing massive environmental damage. The dramatic and dislocating effects of this cycle are often viewed as an inevitable outcome. Remediation is rarely an imperative.

**Left and opposite** The Rufisque Women's Centre in Senegal supports vital social infrastructure – the women's networks that organize schemes ranging from literacy classes to savings cooperatives. The creation of their building involved networks internationally; the work of a Senegalese-Nordic cultural exchange centre and three Finnish architects (see p. 30).

The projects in this chapter demonstrate a new attitude towards the integration, use and reuse of infrastructure in the creation and sustaining of communities. Infrastructure is the framework that supports more transient and varied activity – or grid that can be infilled by social, environmental and economic activities. This is true on a literal level of providing the street and utility grid onto which individual houses or developments attach, and also on a conceptual level of creating a framework for social interaction and the development of renewed communities. To think creatively about infrastructure and to embed new approaches using the very systems that a town or city relies on has the added advantage of mainstreaming creativity, and therefore influencing significant change. The making of infrastructure is a hugely political arena. Because the provision of basic infrastructure (roads, water, etc.) is a fundamental part of shaping a city's plan, to engage citizens of urbanizing settlements (e.g. slums and new towns) with this process makes an important statement about their status as active members of the mainstream community. The projects showcased here address this political and participative issue by proposing not only innovative designs but also new processes for involving the public, reversing in some cases the traditional power balance between deprived communities and the planning process.

A good example of 'slum upgrading' can be found at East Wahdat in Jordan. The new buildings were built on the same sites as the original shacks, ensuring residents did not have to move from 'their' plot as part of a process of legalizing tenure.

This can be as simple as the approach taken in Bester's Camp, South Africa, a township where the process of normalizing the community by providing infrastructure took an unusually sensitive form. In deciding where the new streets should run, the planners themselves walked the site, finding out from residents where the informally agreed boundaries with their neighbours were located, and drawing these on an aerial photograph. The planners then designed the pathways and pegged out the sites based on this working plan, allowing residents a few days to confirm that the pegs were correctly positioned. As a result existing social structures remained intact, contributing to the long-term social stability of the settlement. In East Wahdat in Jordan, the provision of core service units as the first stage in normalizing a slum community was the first step in providing legal tenure for the residents and gaining recognition as citizens with normal rights. The case study Slum Networking (pp. 62–7) demonstrates in detail, and on a large scale, a holistic and innovative solution to the provision of basic infrastructure, bringing together all these issues.

These solutions from the developing world hold valuable lessons for regeneration in the 'first world', where in certain deprived areas there is just as great a need to tackle dislocation, disenfranchisement, social exclusion and outdated infrastructure. Projects like Slum Networking demonstrate a commitment to citizen engagement, building strong social networks around the re-planning process.

The provision of accessible green spaces has become recognized as a key part of the urban infrastructure – the vital 'green lungs' to allow cities some measure of environmental sustainability (absorption of pollutants, sustainable stormwater drainage, offsetting the urban heat island, etc.), as well as social space for the citizens. Xochimilco Park in Mexico City marries an ecological and physical role with the building of social capital and infrastructure (see pp. 56–61). The scheme shows how green infrastructure can redress some of the ecological imbalance of cities alongside providing a holistic response to employment provision, leisure and food production. In Cairo, on top of a centuries-old landfill site, the Aga Khan Foundation has financed the new Al-Azhar Park, built in a city with very little green space per inhabitant. The project includes three massive new water tanks for the city underneath the park. The construction of the park has served as a catalyst for social and economic development and the overall improvement of the quality of life in the district. On a smaller scale, Trees for Cities is planting fruiting orchards on brownfield sites in Addis Ababa, as a way not only to provide much-needed green spaces and to remediate the land, but also to provide employment and support to street children who manage the orchard, harvest and sell the fruit and are thereby able to afford schooling.

The provision of basic infrastructure and services does not need to remain the preserve of the engineer. Artists and other practitioners are increasingly using infrastructure as a tool in the production of creative solutions. Utility NOW! is a small-scale, low-tech, low-cost civic maintenance programme in York, an impoverished town in Alabama. The project grew out of a conversation between the artist Richard Saxton and the mayor and the Public Works department of York about the lack of transportation for city crews to enable them to collect garbage, clean the streets or read meters. Saxton worked with the city and local residents to develop a series of utility tricycles and a community bike repair workshop, housed in a renovated building in the downtown area. In the Rufisque Women's Centre in Senegal (see p. 26), the reading of the role of women as, in a sense, the infrastructure sustaining the society and economy, culminated in a unique partnership between young architects and the local women, resulting in a building to support these social networks that is carefully considered and integrated into the city's fabric.

Problems of infrastructure in the West are often compounded by the pace of industrialization and post-industrial decline, which has left a legacy of severance, redundant forms and contamination. Many cultural projects have begun to use these spaces. The case study Stanica (see pp. 42–8) transcends the conventional 'art factory' approach by inserting new uses into a railway station that still functions as a station, demonstrating how such

The refurbished tricycles of Utility NOW!,
used in street cleaning, show an artist's
approach to the provision of essential services
in the American town of York, Alabama. The
tricycles are stored in a refurbished building
in the town centre which also acts as a
showcase for other appropriate technology
– water collection and reuse, solar heat
collection and energy generation – as well as
a free bicycle repair workshop for the town
where many cannot afford to drive.

existing elements can become the base for broader social and cultural infrastructure. Stanica re-envisions railway stations as multifunctional social hubs that can be the cornerstones of the community, using their location at the junction of road and rail networks to rethink the relationship between this hard and often brutal infrastructure and the social networks that they sustain. The case study of Landschaftspark Duisburg Nord, within the regional vision for the Ruhr Valley in Germany (see pp. 48–55), also demonstrates how infrastructure that has become defunct can become not only the location for new activities but, by the process of its renewal and redevelopment, start to heal the physical landscape and build new social networks.

The long-term investment of infrastructure projects demands huge levels of finance from the authorities mandated with delivery. The projects shown here demonstrate that planning in a participative and democratic way can achieve delivery that is low cost and fast paced. Some of the projects in this chapter are in places of real deprivation, where there are no spare resources for new infrastructure. Lateral, creative solutions have emerged from this context, solutions which maximize benefit through reuse. There is a clear, shared approach behind all these initiatives despite the variety of scale. They all challenge the notion of monofunctional 'neutral' infrastructure and instead push the boundaries hard, making the infrastructure work on many levels that are social, cultural and physical. There is an acknowledgment of the symbolic and cultural value of infrastructure, an awareness that the physical frameworks that support communities can and should contribute to the parallel network of social relationships and active citizenship.

Al-Azhar Park in Cairo has provided a much-need green 'lung' for the city, on top of three massive water tanks, as part of the city's infrastructural upgrading. The site of 74 acres (30 hectares) is located on what was a centuries-old rubbish dump in the middle of the historic old city. However, it has since become controversial by charging an admission fee beyond the means of many local residents. Left, restorers work on the twelfth-century wall uncovered during the construction of the park as part of the project's artisan training and housing restoration programme.

**Playpump is a tool for renewal on many levels. Its impact has perhaps been greater than many 'conventional' renewal strategies, and demonstrates how appropriate, imaginative technology combined with entrepreneurship can be harnessed to provide solutions to seemingly complex problems. Entrepreneurs are rarely included in the development and renewal process, but this case study shows how effective it can be to use a venture capital model to spur innovation and effect social change at low cost.**

**Opposite** A Playpump in action: a social facility and essential physical infrastructure, bringing health, play and clean water to over one million people across South Africa.

The zero-energy pump is a specifically designed playground roundabout that pumps groundwater from boreholes into sealed holding tanks. It is powered by the energy of the children turning the roundabout, keeping costs and maintenance to an absolute minimum, while providing welcome play equipment for children. The low maintenance merry-go-round turns as easily as a standard playground fixture, and over seven hundred have been installed in rural communities in southern Africa.

The Playpump operates on basic windmill equipment which is stocked in cooperative stores throughout Africa and can be found in most other parts of the world as well. Below ground it has only two moving parts but is much more efficient than a traditional hand pump. A typical hand pump installation produces 150 litres (40 US gallons) of water each hour to ground level, where it cannot be stored hygienically. The Playpump can produce 1,400 litres (370 US gallons) of water per hour into an overhead storage tank, and operates at depths from 40 to 100 metres (130 to 330 feet). The 5,000-litre (1,320-US gallon) storage tank is erected on a 6-metre (20-foot) high stand and is a prominent landmark in low-rise villages

# Playpump

South Africa, 1997–ongoing

and townships. It is fitted with four 2- by 3-metre (6- by 10-foot) outdoor advertising signs, resulting in a unique advertising opportunity for the private sector. Two sides of the structure are reserved for public health messages and the others are sold on three-year advertising contracts to companies selling things like soap products and toothpaste, flour and maize, etc. The water pump is a natural gathering point for the women in a community and so it is an excellent place to advertise. Revenue from the advertising pays for the capital cost of the installation and guarantees funds for ongoing maintenance of each Playpump. As a contractual obligation with the advertisers, the sites are serviced at regular intervals for general maintenance on the signage and skilled pump maintenance crews are also included in these visits to the pumps. Local people are trained so that all maintenance and repair work can be carried out by the rural community.

The pump itself was designed by a drilling engineer who struggled to market it, as compared to other mechanical hand pumps it was way too expensive. A marketing executive, Trevor Field, recognized the potential of the idea and designed the tank stand with its advertising hoardings as a way to create extra funding for the pump. Field purchased the patent of the

**Opposite and below** Constructing the Playpumps in a dedicated factory, which provides employment. The pumps are manufactured and installed by local crews set up as independent businesses and trained by Roundabout Outdoor.

**Opposite and above** Playpumps are located near the villages, removing the need for walks of many hours to unreliable and often unsafe waterholes. Through their location, they become social centres and gathering points for the whole community.

pump from the original designer and formed both a non-profit organization to attract funding, and a commercial wing that installs, maintains and sells the advertising space on the tanks. The design of the pump has crucially encompassed not only the physical design but also a creative strategy for funding and maintaining it sustainably.

The provision of water is generally led by technical engineers and is not the realm of 'design'. The award-winning Playpump provides a creative alternative to the major infrastructure upgrading that is a standard part of third-world renewal programmes, saving costs and maximizing benefits to the community in ways that conventional programmes never could – playspace for children, health education and a sustainable maintenance plan. Roundabout Outdoor won a grant from the World Bank for their work and now has international partnerships that will enable it to bring water to ten million people across sub-Saharan Africa by 2010. It shows how a creative, cross-disciplinary design-led approach can lead to a radically different and more appropriate solution, and how entrepreneurs can be used in the renewal process as powerful agents for change.

Stanica demonstrates a uniquely creative approach to integrating infrastructure into the culture and everyday life of a town. It reanimates a neglected but important train station without displacing any of its former uses – and has turned it from a single-use, underinhabited transport building into a cultural centre wholly integrated into the ordinary functioning life of the community.

**Opposite** The opening event celebrating the railway station, using the trains themselves as well as the other parts of the station.

**Below** Stanica brings new life to a major transport interchange at the edge of the old town through a social and cultural programme.

The project, the first of its kind in Slovakia, began to have an enormous impact on cultural policy in the country even before it was completed. By making the space multifunctional, it engages the community on many levels without making demands on their participation, and allows informal, exploratory and gradual discovery of the cultural activities within. Stanica ('station' in Slovak) is the railway station in the town of Zilina, in the north of Slovakia, on a small railway track to Rajec. In 1942, 18,000 to 24,000 Slovak Jews were transported to concentration camps from the station. The present building was constructed in 1946 and was lived in continuously

# **Stanica**
## Slovakia, 2001–ongoing

since then by the Michulek family and their five children. They used to keep domestic animals next to the railway track, and the cherries and strawberries from their garden were renowned throughout the town. In the 1980s, a road overpass surrounded the station building. Squeezed by the industrial scenery, the station started to decay: by 2002, the Michuleks had left and though the train was still operating, train tickets were no longer sold and the building began to fall into disrepair.

The young interdisciplinary cultural organization Truc Sphérique, an NGO linking contemporary arts with social development, came upon the building when they were looking for a new home for their activities. The uniqueness of the project lies in keeping the original function of the building as a railway station, waiting room and ticket office, in connection with space

for creative and social activities. It thus engages children, young people, adults, artists and spectators, and also rail passengers and random passers-by, who might not otherwise encounter cultural activities.

Stanica is a multifunctional, multi-generational space. The times of the events and activities are planned to coincide with the railway timetable so all the communities along the line can observe or participate in the programme. It contains studios for workshops in various fields of art, focusing on non-traditional methods and the engagement of children and young people, and a large space that can be used for performances and conferences. The entrance hall and waiting room carry Slovak and foreign visual artists' exhibitions and documentation of the creative workshops and residential programme. The waiting room functions as a simple railway café for passengers waiting for their train with coffee and regular newspapers,

**Above** Stanica rethinks the function of transport infrastructure as a meeting point and social space.

**Opposite** The station has a unique history but was lying derelict, even when trains were still running.

but has also become a reading room, information centre and internet café, carrying publications about art and culture, information about cultural events and other activities.

The programme includes a residential programme for young artists from Slovakia and abroad to work for one to three months in the ateliers, while schools, children, young people and other visitors can meet the artists at work and discuss their works with them. Truc Sphérique also run an art therapy programme and a volunteering programme, and makes the station available for other groups to hold cultural and social activities, presentations and other events.

The project is conceptually linked to a number of other cultural projects which reuse former industrial buildings and railway stations, but is unique in that it wholly embraces the activities of the station's original function as a given, thereby bringing a richness and vitality that would not exist were the building monofunctional. 'A spectator is not a spectator, a passenger not a passenger and a railway station not a boring place to wait for a train any more.' It is an innovative and imaginative way to weave a long-term, multidimensional cultural programme (the group has signed a thirty-year lease of the building from the rail company) into the life of the town, and the other communities linked by the railway line.

Stanica enables the building to have virtually 24-hour use, better surveillance and a more active presence in the town centre without the imposition of artificial and unsustainable strategies. The project has set up an innovative model for the creation of new cultural centres in Slovakia and other countries, and its approach is transferable and inspirational.

**Left and opposite** A variety of events now take place in and around the building: artist residencies, classes for the community, a café, bookshop, performance spaces and outdoor events.

The Landschaftspark Duisburg Nord, built around a massive disused steelworks, presents a radically different approach to providing essential public green space and leisure facilites. Its long-term planning, cumulative and organic development, use of natural ecological processes and local involvement stand in contrast to the short-term thinking evident in projects on similar sites in the West.

Duisburg Nord also rejects the conception of such projects as architectural showpieces by allowing the landscape, and a diversity of uses, to incrementally transform the site. As a result, it has needed a much smaller budget and is truly integrated into the local community's life. This project sets a new standard for the remediation, reuse and continued management of former industrial complexes. The Ruhr Valley was Germany's industrial

**Opposite** The site of the Duisburg steelworks covers 230 hectares (570 acres). Its regeneration has been centred on the use of natural processes of phytoremediation to decontaminate the land over many years.

**Right** One of the former silos is now used for rock-climbing, managed by a local group.

# Landschaftspark Duisburg Nord

Germany, 1989–ongoing

**Opposite** Public piazzas have been created in the spaces between industrial buildings. The iron plates now used as a centrepiece originally covered the casting moulds.

**Below** The park covers an enormous area of land in one of the most densely populated parts of Europe.

powerhouse, and the Landschaftspark Duisburg Nord occupies the site of a 230-hectare (570-acre) former blast furnace that closed in 1985 after a long period of decline. The park was part of a regional government programme called 'IBA Emscher Park' to encourage economic change and urban development as an impetus to the depressed Ruhr area.

The landscape architects Latz and Partners proposed a series of slow-burn projects that aimed at reanimating the site in collaboration with local residents, and allowing the process to develop as funding was found rather than requiring large initial expenditure. The approach was to use and transform the existing industrial landscape and respect its scale and form, recycling its elements and finding new uses to complement the 'found' spaces of the steelworks. The history of the region was to be celebrated rather than forgotten, enabling the area to regenerate itself slowly and gently without a radical break from its past, which the residents did not want to see discarded. The vital process of decontamination itself was conceived of in the same incremental, long-term way. Rather than expensive decontamination

techniques, plant and tree varieties were chosen for their tolerance of contaminated soil and their ability to naturally purify the industrial waste. Although the most toxic soil had to be sealed and buried in a conventional way, the slag-heaps were seen as craggy mountains to be re-colonized by plants in a gentle and energy-efficient method of decontamination.

The designers considered that new uses and elements would be 'discovered' by the process of starting to test new activities at the site, rather than imposing an overarching programmatic order. The project created a cycle path and promenade along the elevated railway that had previously delivered coal and ore to the furnace; elsewhere a sewage channel was turned into an ecological canal feeding water gardens, powered by a wind power installation in the mill tower, and meditative walled gardens within former silos. Other parts of the park are still in the process of being realized.

The Landschaftspark has been widely admired for its architectural and landscape design. However, unlike showpieces in other cities, it did not aim to base its success on being an international landmark as either a 'set-piece' or a catalyst for cultural tourism and regeneration, which can often be inappropriate or short-term. Instead, it demonstrates that projects can be radical and innovative, contributing in a fundamental way to the

**Above** The development of the park integrated programming with design from the beginning. Imaginative use of the many large spaces creates unexpected opportunities and experiences, such as this orchestral performance.

**Opposite** Dramatic lighting installations celebrate and transform the industrial heritage.

rehabilitation of large and difficult sites, without relying on sweeping changes that dislocate an area and require major capital outlay (with all the attached risks). The realization of the project involved many local groups, including employment schemes for the long-term unemployed. The park's coordinators also encouraged groups to adopt and suggest uses for the industrial buildings, such as scuba diving in a former gasometer and rock-climbing, managed by the German Alpine Club, in former silos. Collaborations also took place with artists such as Jonathan Park (who produced a light installation) and the sculptor Pit Kroke. This boosted a sense of ownership by wider groups, leading to a more self-sustaining process of management and natural evolution of function.

By planning for a long timescale and encouraging the close collaboration of a wide range of local users, this huge area is being gradually and gently transformed. The park management now employs 365 employees which is the equivalent workforce of the operational plant in 1985. Another 260 people work in associated jobs such as gardening, in an educational centre about the building industry and a youth hostel. The German tourist board estimates that the park attracts 300,000 visitors from abroad each year, with a further 230,000 attending special events such as concerts, exhibitions and fairs.

**Xochimilco Park** is an exemplar of a major open-space project serving a megacity – in this case Mexico City. Its programme and design are based on a multidimensional understanding of the city's needs, the local history and context, and a radical ecological agenda on a scale that has a genuine impact on the city.

Mexico City has an estimated population of around 25 million, with this figure doubling every thirty years. It has 1.8 square metres (19 square feet) of green space per inhabitant, well below the World Health Organization recommendation of 9 square metres (97 square feet), and the ground level of the city has sunk by 9 metres (30 feet) during the twentieth century due to the depletion of the natural aquifers. Water resources and adequate storm-water drainage and absorption have become a critical problem due to the rapid urbanization, the drainage of almost all major lakes and watercourses, and the lack of adequate infrastructure.

The 3,000 hectares (7,400 acres) of Xochimilco Park, based around Lake Huetzalin, occupies one of only two areas where examples of the pre-Hispanic technique of 'floating' gardens remain. These gardens – called *chinampas* – are a form of agriculture unique to Mexico and are constructed using willow trees to anchor artificial islands of reeds and organic matter to the base of the lake. This system allows raised ground to be created without

**Left** The new park includes formally designed gardens, but the vast majority is a complex ecosystem of canals and agricultural areas.

**Opposite** Xochimilco Park lies on the outskirts of sprawling Mexico City and contains some of the last natural water resources in the subregion.

# Xochimilco Park

Mexico, 1989–93

**Opposite** Agriculture and nurseries have been restored as the major economic driver of the area.

destroying the fundamental water resource and enables the environment to both absorb and conserve water. Although a UNESCO World Heritage Site, prior to the building of the park urban encroachment, pollution, silting, and underground aquifer depletion had severely degraded the environment. The restoration of the lake and the *chinampas* was seen as a way to have a major impact on the ecosystem of the city.

The creation of the park was a large-scale ecological restoration project including historic restoration, new environmental business and cultural projects. By restoring the *chinampas*, agriculture has been reintroduced to the city, enabling a more sustainable economy and food supply to the local area as well as providing an important 'green lung' for the city, and recreation and educational facilities. The design was guided by hydraulic strategies: water was pumped back into the aquifer to stabilize the site; large reservoirs were created to retain storm water; polluted water was processed at treatment plants; and the treated water was discharged back into the lake to regulate the water levels in the canals. Eroded islands were recreated using meshes of logs filled with dredge and stabilized by willow trees (more than one million trees were planted on the site). Agriculture was reintroduced: some *chinampas* have pastures for grazing and others are planted with flowers and vegetables. A tree nursery on the site now produces 30 million trees every year that are then planted throughout Mexico City. Canals were cleared of harmful vegetation and rehabilitated for recreation as well as agriculture.

The park is viewed as a success from both ecological and urban design perspectives, integrating environmental, historical, agricultural, and recreational uses. The programme includes a centre for environmental education, areas for agricultural research, training courses, a 1,700-stall plant and flower market, organic food stores to increase domestic awareness of food issues, playing fields and sports facilities, and many uses to attract visitors, both foreign and from the city.

Today, pole barges ply the canals of Xochimilco, especially on weekends; gondolas and gondoliers are available for hire at *embarcaderos* built along the edge of the site. Out in the canals, you can collect sustenance for body and soul: kitchen barges sell food, while others ferry professional musicians, available to serenade visitors with romantic songs.

**Opposite** The *chinampas* are effectively floating fields anchored by a grid of trees.

**Below** Sophisticated water management is built into design features and also serves an important function in regulating water levels.

Slum Networking in India demonstrates how an innovative approach to aspects of development as basic and mundane as sewage, water supplies and roads can have a major impact on the social and physical renewal of a city. The thinking and approach of this project has huge relevance not only for developing nations but also for Western cities facing problems of infrastructure and chronic deprivation.

**Opposite** After only five years, the former slum area on the right-hand side of the road is indistinguishable from the 'normal' neighbourhood on the left.

**Below** Slums generally form in the lowest parts of the city, next to watercourses.

**Below right** Himanshu Parikh, the engineer who has developed the Slum Networking method over the last twenty years.

The Slum Networking concept is based on three simple principles. The first is that cities have natural drainage patterns, otherwise they would long ago have drowned in their own waste, and that these can be used as the basis for man-made infrastructure, obviating the need for artificial pumping and deep excavation. Second, it treats the slum dwellers as equal to other citizens, providing them with a quality of services that would be acceptable to any more wealthy resident, thereby assimilating the slum dwellers into the mainstream, demanding a financial contribution from them, ensuring that the projects truly meet their needs and that they put pressure, as stakeholders, on the authorities to maintain the system. The third principle is that providing new physical infrastructure can be a powerful tactic to catalyse wider social and economic change.

# Slum Networking

India, 1987–ongoing

Slum Networking has been developed by the engineer Himanshu Parikh over the last twenty years. It originates from his work in the city of Indore and has been refined and developed since into a sophisticated and sensitive method that is currently being used in cities and villages across India. The projects that have been completed to date have assimilated over one million slum dwellers as full and active citizens and made their slums indistinguishable from 'normal' neighbourhoods. Parikh's design method works with the natural landscape and pattern of development, using the links between the topography and the location of drainage channels, slums and public open spaces to create an organic and sustainable framework to support the city. His observations of the formation of slums and low-income areas revealed that they almost always form near the lowest points of the city, where natural drainage channels occur. By routeing new sewage and water lines just below ground level along these natural paths, they work by gravity rather than requiring pumping stations, as in most Western cities.

By not requiring deep excavation, costs are minimized and the system is easier to maintain. The model also uses a simple but radical design for the new street paving that enables storm water to drain directly into existing waterways rather than into the sewers, conserving water and preventing the sewers overflowing. In almost all cases, careful surveying and subtle re-grading of existing paths and dirt roads means that new routes do not have to be cut through.

**Above** Each family's plot gains a well-built toilet of the same standard as 'normal' houses; further building works to upgrade the home are undertaken at the household's expense.

**Left** The paved roads are easy to clean and at monsoon time drain storm water naturally, with the homes raised above the street to prevent flooding.

**Opposite** Running water is connected to each house, enabling hygienic cooking and washing with research showing huge improvements in health, leading to better access to education and work.

The concept has also reversed any perception of slums as sapping resources from the city. Indian cities generally have inadequate infrastructure for the city as a whole: sometimes less than five per cent of an urban area may have functioning sewage lines. By oversizing the new drainage lines, it was possible to make the networked 'slum' areas the foundation for providing wealthier areas with functioning infrastructure.

The development of the Slum Networking approach has shown that although slum dwellers may live in poverty, they can find financial resources and become active financial partners if given the opportunity. In Indore, the community raised their financial contribution to the project in just three weeks, while it took the municipality over a year to raise the funds. By refusing to treat

deprived communities differently from those seen as more 'capable', the sense of self-esteem and pride in these communities has increased dramatically.

The effects of this radical and equitable approach to the renewal of severely underprivileged communities have been extraordinary. Studies showed that after an initial investment of 4,000 rupees for the infrastructure installation, each household then spent an average of 60,000 rupees on rebuilding their home in a permanent and secure form. Health, education and incomes have improved at faster rates than other programmes targeted specifically at these areas.

The Slum Networking process indirectly achieves many other goals. It impacts on the land rights of the slum dwellers as the municipality must codify their legal status before providing infrastructure for these areas. By stopping waste being discharged into the watercourses, it has been possible to make these areas into valuable public green spaces and fresh-water reservoirs, as well as uncovering important monuments that historically tended to cluster along watercourses. It also makes slum dwellers into taxpayers for the first time by formally acknowledging them as legal residents, as well as participants in the banking system, radically changing their ability to manage and save money.

Slum Networking demonstrates that the design of infrastructure should be given the same level of attention and innovation as architectural design. Infrastructure is a 'common good' that is provided to all regardless of income and has a major part to play in ensuring quality of life and communal pride. Too frequently the design of infrastructure discriminates between the well-off and the disadvantaged through quality of service, maintenance and the location of disruptive major works. Slum Networking's participatory approach to the community as stakeholders, its technical innovation and its locally tailored design are exemplary.

**Opposite** Parikh insists that community leadership is essential for ownership and sustainability. Here a group of women who became involved with the process have gained the skills to now manage many other programmes around the area with a budget of several million rupees per year.

**Above left** Gaining working infrastructure of a standard equivalent to that of other neighbourhoods gives slum dwellers the pride and incentive to improve their own homes.

**Above** Running water also enables entrepreneurship: shops, restaurants and, here, a laundry business.

# CITIZENSHIP

Edible Schoolyard, USA
CLEAN-India, India
Hotel Neustadt, Germany
Ala Plástica, Argentina
De Strip, The Netherlands

Grassroots and political activism over the last forty years has led to a widely accepted consensus on the need for citizens themselves to participate in processes of planning and development. However, this desire to engage citizens is not always accompanied by an understanding of how to engage them effectively, or indeed what the aims of 'consultation', 'participation' or 'public engagement' are. There is still nervousness about the perceived risks of losing control of a project if a 'real' dialogue with the wider community is started, and a concern that engagement will weaken quality or radicalism. This concern can result in the idea that consultation must be carefully managed to get the 'right result'.

In part this is because these terms are often seen as interchangeable and therefore definitions are woolly. But a short-term or limited attitude towards the engagement of citizens increases rather than mitigates the potential for confrontation, and increases the chance of failure as a result. One of the most important principles is to understand and respect the knowledge and expertise in local matters that exists locally and to find the mechanisms to build from them. The projects in this section show how treating a dialogue and collaboration with local communities as the bedrock for a programme of renewal or development can result in outcomes that, far from diluting quality, can be radical and influential in design and impact.

## Consultation, participation or engagement?

Consultation = reactive (opinion sought to test an existing proposal with limitations on range of issues and involvement)

Participation = active (genuine involvement regarding decision-making, small or large)

Engagement = long-term (not a one-off or single-issue orientated)

If the involvement of citizens in processes of urban or rural development is to be sustainable, it must encompass much more than activating respondents in a series of consultations and questionnaires. Encouraging active citizenship is a crucial part of forming strong and stable communities that are able to take the initiative in remedying their own affairs and that are free from constant reliance on external aid. Citizens need to be given the capacity to participate effectively and authoritatively in development and renewal programmes in order to initiate and drive processes of change in partnership, rather than in confrontation, with other agencies and authorities.

The use of consultation as a method of managing opposition and avoiding confrontation denies the potential of an engaged community. This attitude views public participation as a stage in the process rather than an ongoing and positive methodology that can root new developments in the local knowledge, local identity of place, and ensure that new projects truly meet the needs of the local community.

The case studies in this section demonstrate a range of approaches towards empowering and informing lay people to become effective advocates, participants and partners in processes of renewal and development (the 'gate-keepers' or custodians of

The Making Of… is a game devised by cultural planner Hans Venhuizen to mediate the complex conversation between community and commercial interest groups within regeneration. The game is used as a scenario-planner where the complexity of local and national issues are embraced via role play.

demonstrate how the lateral approach and perceived independence of an artist can be a vital tool in encouraging new ways for citizens to engage with each other, as well as their shared spaces. On a larger level, the Kitchener Festival of Neighbourhoods in Canada is an easily replicable, imaginative and effective model for increasing social interaction, dialogue and engagement between the government and its citizens.

In this annual event, organizers encourage citizens to 'invent' their own neighbourhoods consisting of fifty or more adjacent households collaborating in a local project or event and competing for a $10,000 capital improvement award. The events create a new scale of community, encouraging personal rather than institutional relationships, and also enable the city to gain information on citizen priorities, concerns, and thinking on the quality of life in the city. There are physical ramifications to the events that have taken place over the years – one neighbourhood decided to have a backyard music festival, but realized that none of their gardens were big enough, so removed the fences in the neighbourhood to create a communal garden.

The community-building process continues as the winning neighbourhood collectively decides how to use the award. These projects have included a portable skate park, a nature trail in a neighbourhood wood, and an interest-free loan programme to enhance homes in a run-down area. By forging community alliances and encouraging neighbours to get to know one another, the festival has lasting effects on the core of the city's social fabric, as well as providing a way for communities to gain funding for their projects.

Even in the most esteemed and highly valued urban sites, such as Hyde Park or Kensington Gardens in London, artists have been intervening to suggest new opportunities to create and foster social interaction. Public Works' project Park Products developed an alternative economy of social action in the park whereby you were 'rewarded' with a specially designed product produced by students of the nearby Royal College of Art if you volunteered to help a park gardener, introduced yourself to a certain number of strangers and so forth.

Raising the capacity and active citizenship of a community is a long-term process, beginning in school and continuing in an incremental way. Two of the case studies, Edible Schoolyard and CLEAN-India, show how an early engagement with the built environment can be the catalyst for the development of a subtle and important sense of social justice, place and community for young people. CLEAN-India has created a generation of children who are highly skilled environmental advocates and whose dialogue with local governments and physical impact on sites of environmental degradation is extraordinary

**Above and opposite** Public Works' project in Kensington Gardens, London, was produced in collaboration with the park rangers, students from the Royal College of Art, park users and the Serpentine Gallery. It developed a range of prototype products including a 'Chompost Bar' (above), made from compressed compost, litter bags with built-in gloves, a simple bird house and range of jewelry to attract magpies, and a tray for two. These products were then exchanged within a non-monetary economy, and created new social networks within the park.

and inspirational. The project Hotel Neustadt (pp. 88–94), meanwhile, demonstrates how young people can become empowered to take responsibility for changes in their neighbourhood, becoming involved with sophisticated debates around urbanism and social change and producing a programme which can result in long-term shifts in perceptions of place.

The projects highlighted in this section demonstrate tested methodologies of building capacity and ownership within programmes of renewal. However, processes of participation have been central to all the case studies. The aim of local participation and engagement is not simply to ensure a consensus about the form of new development. It is also about creating frameworks in which conflict and difference can be expressed. Active citizenship is central to creating sustainable communities, and it requires the inclusion of communities in decision-making as active players in the game rather than disenfranchised onlookers.

**Left and opposite** FREEmobile was a light but sophisticated project by the artist Jon Rubin in Seattle. The FREEmobile strategically showcased local culture and skills, supported an alternative gift economy, and catalysed new social networks. It was conceived by Rubin to enable residents to share their hobbies, passions and hidden talents. In the summer of 2003 Rubin produced a series of ten weekend events in which different residents drove a customized 1968 Chevy around the neighbourhood distributing goods and services for free.

The Edible Schoolyard addresses several key contemporary social policy agendas in an innovative and creative way. Issues around community cohesion and multiculturalism, public health, education reform and environmental responsibility are all addressed through a visionary yet pragmatic gardening and cooking programme. Through creating a slower, more experiential and less overtly 'skills-oriented' approach to education, it has demonstrated that environmental and social responsibility can be taught to children and have a tangible impact on the community as a whole.

**Above** Working in the kitchen of the Edible Schoolyard

**Opposite** The Edible Schoolyard is an oasis of a very different kind of education that addresses difficult social aims in a lateral and creative way.

The Edible Schoolyard is a non-profit programme located on the campus of Martin Luther King Junior Middle School in Berkeley, California. The cooking and gardening programme grew out of a conversation in 1994 between chef and author Alice Waters, and the then school principal Neil Smith. The school is a state school in a diverse area – forty per cent of the children live at or below the poverty line. It is the designated school in the area for hosting non-English speaking new students, with over twenty ethnicities found in the school.

The programme uses the universal activities of growing food and eating to anchor important and neglected aspects of children's social and environmental education. Understanding these fundamental processes are seen as a way to engage children as citizens with environmental stewardship and responsibility for their own physical health. The Edible Schoolyard is fully integrated into every aspect of the curriculum, from the teaching of history and art through to science and geography, making learning a hands-on, active experience and allowing children to have responsibility for designing and managing a part of their school, while learning how to work together as a community.

The Edible Schoolyard comprises a one-acre organic garden and a specially built 'kitchen classroom', which are used together in the 'Seed to Table' programme. Students participate in every aspect of this process from deciding what to plant and the design of the beds, through caring for and harvesting the produce, and preparing, cooking and eating together in what have become communal rituals for the school. They complete the Seed to Table cycle by taking vegetable scraps back to the garden at the end of

# Edible Schoolyard
### USA, 1994–ongoing

each kitchen class for composting. The experience exposes children to food production, ecology and nutrition, and fosters an appreciation of fresh and natural food and meaningful work. In a community where many students lack a settled home life and adult leadership, the programme also allows students to gain less tangible social skills such as respect for others, team working, conversation and appreciation for beauty. For many students, the meals in the kitchen classroom are the only meals they eat in the company of others.

All 950 students participate in the Edible Schoolyard for a large proportion of their school schedule. The staff's vision was to make Edible Schoolyard activities an extension of students' regular classroom education, not a separate experience. Teachers use garden and kitchen activities as common reference points to activate prior knowledge and specific lessons that meet the California Content Standards. Some examples include compost and worm lessons, links to the Landforms science curriculum, plant structure and function, and ecology. State Standards in world history, English, and reading are dealt with in the kitchen classroom lessons. Students spend up to six hours a week in the garden or kitchen – four 90-minute double lessons – in the sixth grade, and up to three hours a week in the eighth grade.

The Edible Schoolyard's principles are now being applied across all Berkeley public schools in a new School Lunch Initiative which provides a healthy lunch made from local produce for all 10,000 students. It applies the Edible Schoolyard model of experiential learning rather than take-it-or-leave-it 'healthy' options to encourage and nurture children's understanding of the

importance of what they eat. The project is a partnership of the Chez Panisse Foundation and the Berkeley Unified School District, in collaboration with the Centre for Ecoliteracy and the Children's Hospital Oakland Research Institute.

**Opposite** The Edible Schoolyard is planned every year by the students and forms a core part of the curriculum.

**Left** Hand-made signs waiting to be placed in the garden.

**Above** Children discover the surprise and pleasure of growing and harvesting, alongside scientific skills and cultural understanding.

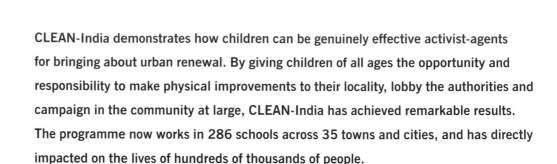

CLEAN-India demonstrates how children can be genuinely effective activist-agents for bringing about urban renewal. By giving children of all ages the opportunity and responsibility to make physical improvements to their locality, lobby the authorities and campaign in the community at large, CLEAN-India has achieved remarkable results. The programme now works in 286 schools across 35 towns and cities, and has directly impacted on the lives of hundreds of thousands of people.

In a country where natural resources are vast but the pressures of rapid development and a population explosion mean that there is little care for ecological impact, CLEAN-India aims to change fundamentally people's attitudes towards their environment. It trains schoolchildren to become the environmental activists and advocates in their communities, monitoring air quality, trees and green spaces, water quality and other environmental indicators, and proposing remedial actions within their community and to the local authorities, as well as carrying out physical projects themselves. Each school operates relatively independently, with programmes adapted to the area's context and community, but are linked in a network to share methods, information and resources. The children are empowered to lead their own programmes rather than being 'led' by adults, and leave the programme as knowledgeable, committed activists for the environment.

Students of member schools are trained in scientific skills for monitoring environmental quality using field-based kits specially designed for the project. This empowers them to learn more about the quality of the environment and use their findings to create or demand solutions. They use the Geographical Information System to chart these on a publicly accessible map and their findings are validated by recognized research institutions.

**Left** Schoolchildren are at the core of the CLEAN-India programme, organizing their peers and taking the initiative for action.

**Opposite** One of the most widespread citizen campaigns of recent years was for better air quality, in which CLEAN-Delhi played a major role. All buses in Delhi now run on low-emission fuel.

The students then carry out physical projects to improve their local environment, both within and outside their schools (which have up to 4,000 pupils). These range from converting their schools to zero-waste schools and installing water harvesting systems, to tree planting, waterways cleaning, and other greening activities in public spaces, waste dumps and local rivers. Students have also designed and installed rainwater harvesting systems, recycling and composting units, and water filtration units in temples and apartment blocks, for the benefit of whole communities.

A crucial part of the students' work is generating awareness within the wider community. This may involve personal pressure on their families, slum adoption programmes, working with low-income groups, formation of action groups and campaigning for change at local authority level.

Students have also initiated programmes with slum dwellers and rag-pickers, teaching them to make saleable products out of recycled waste and eco-friendly items such as natural pigments, and training them in methods to purify water, manage and recycle waste, and conserve natural resources.

The methods used by the students to improve their environment, such as specially designed paper recycling equipment, composting units and water purification methods, have had an impact beyond the schoolroom. The Delhi Secretariat now uses the paper recycling equipment developed by CLEAN-India to recycle all its paper waste, creating jobs in the process. Equally, the campaigns led by the children have had a major impact on changing policy and forcing the relevant authorities to take action. Their voices have been instrumental in changes including the conversion of Delhi's

**Opposite** Students monitor the quality and quantity of green spaces and report breaches of environmental guidance.

**Right** A current campaign is to clean up the polluted Yamuna river, where schoolchildren monitor the water quality and regularly report to and lobby the authorities.

**Below** The paper recycling equipment specially designed for CLEAN-India is now used by the Delhi Secretariat to recycle all its paper in-house.

**Below right** Students conducting water purity tests after a field trip.

**Opposite** School children conduct regular fieldwork and involve communities through educating and creating simple solutions for issues such as water filtration and waste recycling.

public transport to low-emission compressed natural gas (CNG) fuel, the promotion of bio-fuels by the Forestry Department in Kurnool, and tree-planting policies. Some CLEAN-India schools also collaborate with local authorities, for example in monitoring the survival rate of Delhi's tree-planting programme.

The projects that the students have initiated have had an enormous impact on the urban landscapes of the thirty-five cities in which the programme operates – in Delhi the programme has been instrumental in the increase in the city's green cover from 10 to 18 per cent between 2001 and 2005. Most importantly, the programme is training a generation of children, from good educational backgrounds and who are likely to become the next generation of leaders, to understand the relationship between urbanism and the environment in a sophisticated and radical way.

Hotel Neustadt was a temporary project in Halle in former East Germany initiated by a young people's theatre company and an architecture practice, and implemented by over one hundred young people. It demonstrates how temporary creative projects can engage and excite, alter preconceived perceptions and transform the image of the most difficult and deprived areas in ways that have a long-term effect.

Halle-Neustadt was the second largest socialist housing estate in the GDR, planned in the 1960s and built over twenty-five years. Using 'modern' construction methods, an international staff of architects and town planners created a city for 100,000 chemical factory workers in the area. It was fully equipped with social and urban infrastructure – supermarkets, kindergartens, schools, playgrounds, restaurants, a large-scale city centre, shops, a cinema and a city council. But the radical changes in the German economy meant that by autumn 2003 the chemical factory had closed, one third of the apartments were vacant, unemployment was running at 25 per cent, and schools and shops were empty.

Hotel Neustadt originated as a summer project for teenagers in the Thalia Young People's Theatre to create an environment where young people could explore ideas of relevance to them, particularly their future as adults and their housing situation. It was conceived as a place for teenagers to test ideas, lead and carry out their own projects and, perhaps, even live for a while. The proposal to use the abandoned buildings of Halle-Neustadt came from research that the architecture practice Raumlabor had been doing on the area for the city government.

**Above left** The project resulted in the creation of a fully functioning hotel with all the traditional services, including a hotel taxi.

**Opposite** Halle-Neustadt was an East German new town originally built to house workers in a nearby chemical factory.

# Hotel Neustadt
Germany, 2002–2003

The project involved the renovation by teenagers of an abandoned building as a fully functioning hotel and the invitation of artists to carry out temporary installations and art projects in the building and surrounding area. The free use of the building was negotiated with the owner, a private property developer, and the railway station became a cultural centre for events with its former café as the project's offices. Early workshops in schools and liaison with teachers, as well as events in the train station and the project office, attracted many teenagers who wanted to participate in the project, and allowed the residents of the area to start engaging with the project and to get used to the concept of a major arts festival taking place in these abandoned spaces.

Ninety-two rooms on eight out of eighteen floors were renovated. The 'Neustadt show' involved more than sixty participants who stayed in the hotel while developing a game-based circuit for visitors to the rest of the tower block. These included Kyong Park's 'Big Slide', a mini-golf course on the fifth floor, a programme working with current residents of Neustadt on renovating and rethinking their balconies, and also the updating of the text 'Cities Make People' which was written when the new town was originally built. A week-long theatre festival took place, alongside music, films, a bar, a restaurant and other events.

**Opposite** The station and the square outside became a focus of activity, with installations, concerts and events including rap battles between local teenagers, which engaged kids with the project at the start.

**Right** The hotel functioned as a conventional high-rise hotel, with reception, tourist information and cycle hire, but all organized and staffed by teenagers.

The impact of Hotel Neustadt was important both for the teenagers involved but also for the city as a whole, and the discussion about how areas like Halle-Neustadt could be regenerated. The mayor and council of Halle stayed in the hotel and gave the project substantial political support. Over 8,700 visitors from all over the world came to the festival over the two months, engaging the town in international debates about shrinking cities and urban change. The area is now increasingly used for cultural events, demonstrating how temporary events can reanimate and provoke positive debate and engagement both by the local community and by a wider international audience of leading practitioners and thinkers. On a more intimate scale, the engagement of the next generation of residents in the area has led many of the young people involved to engage in entrepreneurial activity of their own – setting up film or arts companies, running bars and other businesses – and contributing in a very direct way to the regeneration of the area.

**Left** Three of the bedrooms in the hotel, decorated by the teenagers and with furniture made from reused timber to a bespoke design.

**Opposite** New social networks emerged through the programme. Here local residents help out with the refurbishment and redecoration.

The work of artist collective Ala Plástica in Argentina may be visible only on a micro-scale but it incorporates an impressive bioregional vision focusing on major strategic work with local communities as well as direct actions and built interventions.

This study demonstrates how a group of independent practitioners can be effective communicators between communities and authorities at a high level. Through their advocacy, networking and live projects, the group has linked together organizations from UNESCO to small community groups to realize creative social and environmental projects in the delta of the Rio de la Plata.

The Rio de la Plata estuary forms the final stage of a water system of the Paraná/Plata basin, second only to the Amazon basin in its importance for South America. It covers Brazil, Paraguay, Uruguay, Bolivia and Argentina.

**Right** Ala Plástica works in small and incremental ways with the local community institutions of the delta.

**Opposite** The Rio de la Plata delta drains much of South America, linking diverse ecosystems.

# Ala Plástica

Argentina, 1995–ongoing

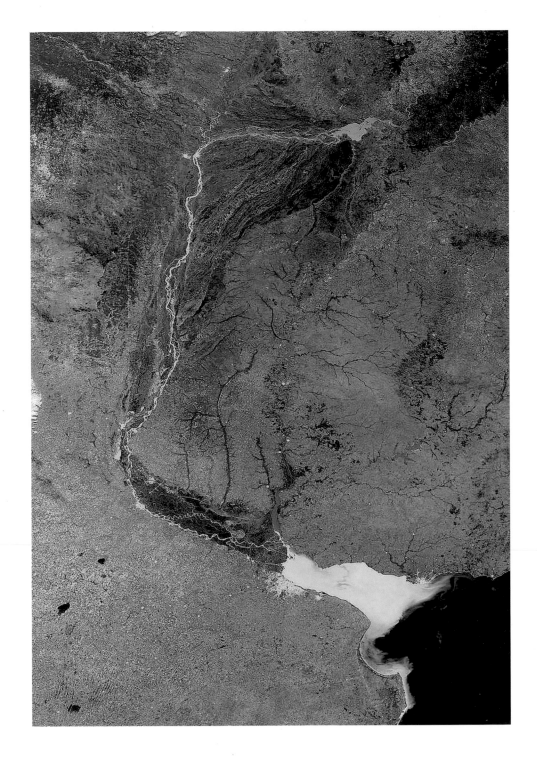

The estuary is the main source of fresh water for over 11 million people settled in only 60 kilometres (38 miles) along its Argentine riverside. This mega-urban settlement (Greater Buenos Aires) is the place where in the 1970s as many as 30,000 people 'disappeared' under the military government's control, in an attempt to crush emergent social movements, growing claims for social justice and active attitudes of solidarity. The area is also one of the most polluted urban areas in the world.

Ala Plástica is a cross-disciplinary collective that links ecological, social and cultural programmes. The Bioregional Initiative grew out of a field project on degraded natural reedbeds, aiming to revive this naturally occurring ecosystem which filtered sewage and other impurities from the water. Ala Plástica initiated a process of communication between local stakeholders for coastal social and environmental reclamation (NGOs, government officials, scientists, local communities) in a local forum to discuss the human–ecological relationship around the Rio de la Plata and to activate

local participation in the monitoring and evaluation of this biogeographically fragile landscape.

The Bioregional Initiative focuses on coastal communities, providing links and networks among different groups working on local development objectives. Following documentation of the range of ideas for change generated by the forums, coordination of a programme included implementation of alternative energy schemes, public intervention in urban/rural regeneration, the establishment of biodiversity corridors, integrated productivity, control of erosion, reforestation, soil and riverside protection, and flood defence.

One of their biggest projects involved remediation and public information work around a major Shell oil spill in 1999. Within a month of the spill, Ala Plástica carried out an analysis of the situation, including a field survey, and aerial and satellite imagery analysis in partnership with the local

**Above** A reed plantation by the river in the La Plata port area.

**Opposite above** Rubén Leron, a willow farmer and local partner of Ala Plástica. With the organization's support, he has become a key player in relaunching willow farming in the Punta Lara area.

**Opposite** Rubén Leron overseeing a willow-planting workshop with high school students.

government and UNESCO. The survey team included local riverside workers (reed harvesters, fishermen, scientists), a fauna rescue group linked to La Plata City Zoo and an information team, which released public documents about the oil spill on a daily basis.

Ala Plástica succeeded in winning the support of UNESCO, thus creating a dynamic relationship between local knowledge and a global institution. Through projects such as these, Ala Plástica is successful in intervening directly in remediation work while also contextualizing issues at a global level and therefore supporting wider public debates.

The current major project under the Bioregional Initiative is Project
AA, which addresses the effects of flooding on the vulnerable communities
of the region. The group has built emergency 'lodges' for flood-prone
communities, which act as community centres and ecological research
stations. They have also constructed embankments and other protection
for school buildings and run training programmes for communities on
community farms and local crafts skills. Members of the group now sit on
the Environmental Advisory Council of Buenos Aires State and the La Plata
Commission for the Environment. The group has also established cooperative
agreements on environmental education with La Plata National University.

Ala Plástica has succeeded in forming powerful partnerships through
its networking and advocacy, while protecting the interests of communities
lacking a coherent voice. Its value lies also in its long-term commitment to
the area and the communities, over many years acting as a consistent point of
contact in a changing political scene. This commitment has enabled it to gain
the genuine trust of the communities, and Ala Plástica's success in achieving
small but significant physical interventions, levering funding from diverse
sources, has demonstrated its capacity to create meaningful change.

**Opposite** Involving communities in the clean-
up of rare marshlands, engaging them with
ecological and territorial issues.

**Above left** The integral Nature Reserve of
Punta Lara, where Ala Plástica has been
helping to strengthen local interest and
generating strategic visions for its future.

**Above** One of Ala Plástica's recent projects
has been to provide flood-prone communities
with protection and raised emergency 'lodges'
which also act as community centres.

Focused on a row of previously abandoned shops, De Strip evolved from a long-term commissioning programme of artist projects embedded in a major urban renewal scheme. Over a two-year period it enabled a community to participate in communal activities while their area underwent massive change. By offering a range of spaces and ways for residents to meet each other, it allowed them to join together in facing the changes around them, and provided a positive outlet and voice for the diverse cultural identities that make up the area. The whole ten-year commissioning programme, Until We Meet Again, is an outstanding example of how long-term cultural and creative programmes can accompany major urban redevelopment as a way to allow residents to comment on the process of change.

In 1995 artist Jeanne van Heeswijk was commissioned to develop a project that centred on the redevelopment of the Westwijk area in the city of Vlaardingen near Rotterdam. Westwijk was a new quarter of 20,000 inhabitants built between 1951–61 whose entire building stock was being redeveloped over a ten-year period. Jeanne chose to invite several artists, architects and designers over a period of ten years to organize 'meetings' in active cooperation with the inhabitants, naming the programme Until We Meet Again. The artists created temporary sculptures, projects, installations and happenings, each aiming to contribute to the involvement of the inhabitants with the changes that were taking place within the redevelopment of Westwijk.

Within this wider cultural programme the largest housing association in the area, and the landlords of fifteen vacant shops at centre of Vlaardingen, commissioned van Heeswijk to consider a new use for this strip of disused shops, which were attracting vandalism and arson. They asked van Heeswijk to conceive of a new, temporary function for what had, until recently, been a strip of shops, including a supermarket, a bakery, a flower shop and a drugstore. The new centre opened to residents in May 2002 for eighteen months, delivering three main elements: an exhibition programme, the provision of artists' workspaces, and a community programme along with a video-production facility. The inhabitants of Westwijk also programmed an ongoing series of activities in the museum café.

# De Strip
## The Netherlands, 2002–2004

**Above** De Strip became a fixed point of reference through the disorientating process of demolition and redevelopment that happened around it.

**Opposite** The strip of abandoned shops prior to their transformation.

For the exhibitions programme, a branch of the internationally prestigious Boijmans van Beuningen Museum was established within three of the former shops to exhibit work from its collection of applied and modern art. A museum bookshop and café were also installed. In the former supermarket showroom, cultural collective Showroom MAMA organized a series of workshops and exhibitions on youth and street culture. Artist Peter Westernberg created *Het Uit+Thuis* video-magazine, a space and online TV-channel for watching and making video.

Artists and craftsmen were offered studios and workspaces for a period of three months at a time. No rent was charged on the condition that the tenants opened their studios to the public twice a week and ran workshops for interested local residents. A bi-monthly newsletter in the form of a comic strip not only updated residents on the programme's agenda but also provided a forum for discussion of De Strip and the development of Westwijk as a whole.

In response to the fact the shopping centre was no longer used for direct economic production, the De Strip project demonstrates the great value of cultural production to the maintenance of the local community infrastructure. The programme was extremely popular with the community and as a result it was extended for six months longer than envisaged. The programme transformed the precinct without losing its centrality to the

**Left** Classes, exhibitions and local events were held on a constantly changing programme, animating the space.

**Opposite** The team of local volunteers brought together by the project dismantling the building, with its iconic red façade, at the end of the two-year programme.

community at large and with the local residents' full participation. It used cultural and creative activities inventively, as a way to encourage self-expression and communal interaction, without ever resorting to trite or patronizing cliches of 'community art', by involving the highest quality of artists and practitioner, and constantly pushing for imaginative, radical approaches.

**Opposite** The 'Giant of Vlaardingen', an installation built by artist Florentijn Hofman, working with the community, as part of De Strip's programme.

**Above and left** Artists were given studio space on condition that they opened to the public or ran events twice a week.

# RURAL

Nelson Mandela Museum, South Africa
Now Here: A Park for Las Aceñas, Spain
Rural Studio, USA
Cattle Tracks, Spain

Regeneration and renewal are not just urban processes. The issues facing rural areas are as pressing as those facing towns and cities, and in many ways more so. The decline of traditional agriculture and rural industries in the West, and the massive pressures on the environment to support the population explosion in the developing world means that rural areas are changing their structure and way of life dramatically.

In the West, the changing use of rural land is a heavily political issue as economies, demographics and social hierarchies alter rapidly. The globalization of food production, the sudden death of the village in Europe, and the dangerous sterility of mass agriculture all mean that rural areas are facing instability on a huge scale. There are similarities here with the situation in developing nations, where the balance of power has also altered in favour of the cities, which nevertheless rely on rural areas to support their needs of food, energy, construction materials and water. The impact of the low-density peri-urban sprawl, devoid of identity, means that there is a rapidly growing nowhere land, a new phenomenon of the twenty-first century.

Rural settings have often been discounted as sites of conservatism that refuse to accept change or modernity, but some of the most radical projects and thinking,

historically and in recent years, have come from rural places. Rural areas have in fact traditionally been the sites for utopian visions and experimentation – whether model villages in Europe, or the radicalism of the Barefoot College in India which deliberately works in an area which is 'remote, inaccessible and very difficult physically to reach so that there is peace, mental space and non-interference from so-called experts'. Similarly, there are a growing number of eco-villages across sub-Saharan Africa that have developed as a response to the desire for self-sufficiency. These projects demonstrate how rural areas can provide the space for plural visions and heterotopias, and all crucially share a desire for independence and devolution, and make the creation of a specifically rural infrastructure a key aim.

**Above** Druk White Lotus School in Ladakh, Nepal – a beacon project developing appropriate technology for remote rural areas.

**Opposite** The MILK-project in Latvia tracked processes of trade across Europe, highlighting the unseen contribution that rural economies make.

In the work of Rural Studio the distinctiveness and specificity of the rural environment led to a particular approach to education and social architecture. This radical approach relies on the aspects of closeness and integration of rural communities rather than that of isolation. The Rural Studio, which works in the poorest counties of one of the poorest states of the USA, vividly demonstrates the impact of context-based education in a deprived community. It is a pre-eminent model for how an academic institution can work in its community, but its key lesson is in the way it has embedded itself into the place, creating a new relationship on both a practical and a humanist level between creative practice and the unique social and physical character of the local area.

The case studies in this section demonstrate new strategies for protecting or retaining fragile rural ecosystems, including the social and economic infrastructure of dispersed communities. They share a concern with these underlying issues and all appear to seek a way of tracing, confirming, bolstering and making that infrastructure more explicit.

The project at Osuna, Spain, for example, renovates an ancient system of connectivity, the cattle tracks, to underpin economic development (see pp. 136–41). This renovation of the cattle tracks is an elegant and subtle intervention which provides benefits to local people as well as to visitors and tourists and demonstrates that it is possible to use a heritage asset to provide a platform for new economic development which resists the increasingly prevalent theming of the rural environment.

The Nelson Mandela Museum (see pp. 116–21), spread across three sites in South Africa, takes a lateral dispersed approach to creating a museum that makes the strategic thinking of Western institutions pale in comparison. It is a radical interpretation of a polycentric programme, that in each of the three sites provides social infrastructure opportunities for rural communities – for example, a water pump at Mvezo and sporting activities at Qunu. This is not a conventional take on how and where to house a collection of artefacts but rather a re-envisioning of a memorial as an active ongoing contributor to the community.

In Europe in recent years, artists, curators and commissioners have increasingly worked with the rural as a site of critical practice, shedding light on the decline of and intervening within traditional rural structures. The analysis of devolution and distributed networks in MILK-project, by two artists (one Dutch, one Latvian), worked against the isolation of rural communities, making visible the line of production of milk in Latvia to the distribution networks in western Europe. By tracking and disseminating information about this cross-border economic infrastructure, strategic connections between isolated 'foreign' communities became linked and the critical investigators, the artists Esther Polak and Ieva Auzina, reframed a rural geography. New networks for dispersed practitioners are also required, this forms part of the mission of the artists' collective myvillages.org, founded by Wapke Feestra, Kathrin Böhm and Antje Schiffers, which was established to create the space for an investigation into practitioners who were brought up in rural villages and how this relates to contemporary contextual art practice.

**Above and opposite** This building by architect Jae Cha in Bolivia uses the simplest technology to create a tiny but important intervention in a fragile community. Its simple space means that it can function variously as church, marketplace and day-care centre. The architecture works with the particularities of the local climate and uses the potential of self-build to support the local social infrastructure.

Rural areas face challenges that are particular and unique. The balance between landscape and communities in rural areas means that the social and natural ecosystems are more delicate than in urban areas. Issues of heritage and tradition are central, as in virtually every country the rural or village culture contains the roots of national myth, communal identity and idyll. The absence of choice or diversity means that one action can have a massive effect, as evidenced by the closure of the tannery in Las Aceñas, which forms the backdrop for the case study Now Here (see pp. 122–5) where art replaced industry as a key economic and social engine for a small village.

Rural areas are the sites not only for innovative planning but for a new level of entrepreneurship and invention. We have already seen the South African Playpump, an example of how a design-led, simple innovation can play a huge part in addressing pressing issues in rural areas. The entrepreneurship of Playpump creates practical yet playful physical infrastructure tailored to the off-grid needs of rural communities in a way that also meets needs for community gathering spaces and the dissemination of vital health information. Boundaries are blurring, and 'peri-urban' fringe areas where urban, suburban and rural disintegrate are ever increasing. These areas require a special sensitivity to local conditions: a delicate ecology, that can build upon the specificity and the distinctiveness. Because of the timescale of ecological change, the quickening pace of social generational changes, and the links to changing economic circumstances, a consideration of long-term planning is especially important in rural areas. The links between the past and a new longer-term vision of the future based on the distinctiveness of the local culture and communities is a strong overarching theme of these case studies.

Vistula Now! is a project started by Jacek Bosek, an environmentalist and community activist, to preserve the ecological richness and diversity of the Vistula River, the largest in Poland. His approach is highly multi-disciplinary, encompassing government lobbying, masterplanning, citizen actions, festivals and cultural performances. The approach taken by Bosek's organization, Klub Gaja, has been to engage the communities around the river and by generating a sense of civic pride in its ecosystem, create a commitment to save it. Klub Gaja runs a comprehensive public education and outreach programme, including training for volunteers who seek to educate their neighbours about why it is critical to preserve the river. To date, the programme has recruited over 400 volunteers, with Klub Gaja chapters in more than nineteen Polish communities. Klub Gaja publishes a regular newsletter that provides up-to-date information and helps to unite the groups of volunteers into a cohesive national movement. Bosek's approach sets out to tackle the generic and particular problems of rural areas in an ambitious and strategic way.

3 Rivers 2nd Nature (3R2N) was a five-year project initiated in 2000 by artists working through an academic research facility, the STUDIO for Creative Inquiry at Carnegie Mellon University in the USA. The project aimed to address the meaning, form and function of the three rivers and 53 streams of Allegheny County, Western Pennsylavania. Like Vistula Now! it takes a large-scale, interdisciplinary, long-term approach to cultural and environmental remediation.

**Above and opposite** Direct activism of Klub Gaja in Poland, campaigning for the Vistula river. The Vistula river is perhaps Europe's last natural river – one whose course has not been altered by man – with a continent-wide ecological importance. The approach taken by Klub Gaja has been to engage the communities around the river and, by generating a sense of civic pride in its ecosystem, to create a commitment to save it. This includes a comprehensive public education and outreach programme, including a training programme for volunteers who educate others in their communities. Opposite is a mural by Klub Gaja on a bridge over the river.

The project offers a platform for creative dialogue about the conditions of the waterfront. The 3R2N team advocated that empirical study can inform discussions about public experience, perception and value and that an artistic approach can offer solutions which may not have been reached through conventional methods or institutions. The team proposed radical planning to support a restorative approach to the physical redevelopment, in both aesthetic and ecological terms. The goal was to develop the scientific tools to enable this approach. Interdisciplinary teams focused on terrestrial and aquatic issues as well as community dialogue and planning. The teams included artists, architects and historians from Carnegie Mellon University. Additional members of the team included environmental scientists, biologists, geologists and a conservation planner from other nearby universities and private practice. Experts in regional and state regulatory interests served on a technical advisory committee while non-profit organizations formed the basis of an outreach advisory board. The project team developed rigorous field methods to gather scientific data to inform understanding of the existing river conditions, conducted a computer mapping analysis of each subject area to understand the forces affecting water quality, botany, biodiversity, public access, use and bank conditions, and examined historical material to understand the rivers and the range of human activities

that have influenced their change over time. Using these tools, 3R2N has sought to identify the potential for preservation and restoration of natural and cultural systems.

The rural is becoming a site of critical interest for planners and politicians – in the West as agriculture declines while pressure for development increases; and in developing nations as mass migration from rural to urban areas coincides with the need for massively more productive systems of agriculture in order to feed an exploding population. Practitioners and thinkers are beginning to redress the imbalance between urban and rural. No longer can the assumption be made that all creative practitioners leave their rural birthplace and head for a big city – the increasing anonymity of urban areas has found its mirror in the increasing importance attached to place and roots, and the more sensitized understanding of distinctiveness that exists in rural areas. As the debate widens in the wake of the global impact of super- and mega-cities, there is an increasing interest in the often radical projects that have been based in rural areas but that have often been overlooked by the urban academic and practitioner classes. The case studies in this chapter are in some ways a call for further recognition that, in many cases, rural communities are far more radical in their desires than urbanites – and that one of the key sites for finding real social engagement in development is rural.

**Below** The site of the 3 Rivers 2nd Nature project near Pittsburgh, Pennsylvania, USA, is a landscape of former industrial activity that cannot now be classified as either entirely rural or entirely urban. The interdisciplinary project studies the changing ecologies of the brownfield land and works with local stakeholders to develop new strategies for remediation.

The Nelson Mandela Museum is a radical redefinition of a museum as a decentralized, community-orientated project. Mandela specifically wanted this museum to be of primary benefit to the community and not to serve as a frozen shrine to his achievements. The conventional concept of cultural or heritage facilities has been rejected – instead, the Museum is understood as an ongoing process that serves as a means to develop basic community infrastructure, and to further social organization through maximizing job creation, training and educational functions. The development of the brief and built form of the museum has involved a rich investigation into the landscape and history of the area, its craft traditions and culture.

**Opposite** The new Youth and Heritage Centre at Qunu, housing a skills training and cultural programme.

**Below** Mandela's aim for the museum was to impact proactively on the culture and communities of the area and not to act as a static memorial.

The museum is comprised of three buildings in three different towns within a 40-kilometre (28-mile) radius. In Umtata, the regional capital, the imposing Bhunga building has been reused and now houses the awards and gifts given to Mandela, as well as an exhibition of the story of his life. This building was once the seat of the colonial government and during the period of apartheid it was used by the legislative assembly of the Transkei, which makes it a potent container for the documentation of the struggle against apartheid. The second element is in Mvezo (see pp. 118–19), an almost deserted village and the birthplace of Mandela where, in the 1960s, the government forcibly resettled the population. It contains an open-air display and heritage centre and plans exist to preserve the circular foundation walls of the dwellings. In the rural community of Qunu, where Mandela spent his early childhood, there is a Youth and Heritage Centre comprising a community cultural facility and a skills training programme for the community.

Job creation and economic development opportunities for local people have been fundamental concerns in the conceptualization of the project. This has meant the creation of new jobs, particularly for women, in the form of short-term work in building construction and long-term employment in the field of tourism. The application of local craft traditions – in making wattle fences and screens, and the use of masonry techniques, for example – has allowed for a variety of skilled and unskilled local labour to be employed. In response to the urgent need to provide basic infrastucture to remote and marginalized communities, this dispersed 'museum' also includes communal

# Nelson Mandela Museum
## South Africa, 1997–2006

**Above and opposite** The information stand and marker at Mandela's birthplace, Mvezo, also provides clean water and a meeting point for the community.

**Right** Moshile Nompoko, a traditional storyteller at Mvezo. The Museum promotes ancient ways of passing on knowledge alongside more contemporary displays.

facilities such as simple structures to create shaded meeting points, and water standpipes and washing places to bring clean water to the community.

The information stand at Mvezo forms a striking starting point for the rural tour, which traces the life of Nelson Mandela and 'the long road to freedom'. A raised timber walkway and a stone platform are distinguished from the visitors' paths as newly created places of contemplation. In addition, a reservoir and a shaded washing facility have been built, where the people of the scattered villages in the area can come together. Before the creation of these amenities, the villagers had to fetch water in canisters from the river.

The Qunu component of the museum, the Nelson Mandela Youth and Heritage Centre, functions as the main educational focus. It accommodates economic development and job creation activities including craft production, sewing, and so forth, but principally is comprised of facilities for young people. The programme includes after-school activities as well as holiday youth camps where education and recreation programmes aim to equip youth with leadership and life-skills, instil a sense of civic and community awareness, and engender an understanding and appreciation of nature and the environment. The activities also aim to instil an awareness of indigenous

phila kwam ndaye ndazinikela kulo mzabalazo
During my lifetime I have dedicated myself to this
u abaNtsundu. Ndilwele ingcinezelo ngabantu
struggle of the African people. I have fought
diyilwele nengcinezelo ngabantu abaNtsundu.
against white domination, and I have fought
nombono entliziyweni yam, umbono wesizwe
against black domination. I have cherished the
esilawulwa ngemo yedemokhrasi, apho bonke
ideal of a democratic and free society in which all
ye ngemvisiswano, futhi bonke benamathuba
persons live together in harmony and with equal
ni. Lo ke ngumbono endithemba ukuwuphilela
opportunities. It is an ideal which I hope to live
numeza. Kodwa ke ukuba ngaba kuyimfuneko,
for and to achieve. But if needs be, it is an ideal
ngumbono endizimiseleyo ukuwufela.
for which I am prepared to die.

culture and heritage and create among urban youth a sensitivity to the challenges and hardships facing rural communities.

The Nelson Mandela Museum has had a major impact not only on the tourism economy but also on the daily life and access to opportunities for local people. It demonstrates how cultural facilities do not have to conform to the 'iconic' model in order to catalyse regeneration but instead can provide vitally needed community facilities and raise the profile of the area. By decentralizing the museum experience to three very different locations, the museum not only has a distinct identity but also provides a unique visitor experience, allowing tourists an insight into rural life in the Eastern Cape, while strengthening the local communities' capacity to become sustainable without losing their unique culture and connection to the land.

**Above and opposite** The museum in Umtata now houses the main archive and exhibition of Mandela's life, within the symbolically important surroundings of the former parliament building.

**Now Here is a project by the multidisciplinary group c a l c in the small northern Spanish village of Las Aceñas, where the group is based. c a l c undertook to redefine a centre for the village, left void after the closure of a tannery that had been both the economic and the cultural heart of the community.**

Now Here is a small-scale project, but demonstrates the lightness and simplicity of intervention that is appropriate to the delicate social and cultural ecology of rural areas. It is acupunctural, using small means to create an impact on the community that is perhaps immeasurable. The relationship between c a l c, the creative practice who carried out the project, and the residents of Las Aceñas, in Asturias, resulted in a sensitive and pragmatic intervention. Now Here demonstrates how alternative processes that might seem 'outside' the practice of regeneration or development can be used to directly fund and enable regenerative change, bypassing conventional and often bureaucratic routes.

The project came about when c a l c was invited to participate in the exhibition 'Things between life, art and work' at the O.K Center for Contemporary Art in Linz, Austria. After deliberating on the form of their contribution, c a l c decided to 'tap into the wire of cultural transformation and reroute some of Linz's richness to where we were from' – Las Aceñas, Spain. The group decided to test whether the methodology of art production and the art economy could provide the financial and practical framework for a change at the local level of their small community. Las Aceñas had grown around a leather tanning factory, which was physically at the heart of the village. With the disappearance of this small industry the village centre became obsolete as the factory was not only the economic but also the cultural core of Las Aceñas, providing social structure, organizing events and acting as the focus for communal gatherings and activity. Requests by the community for improvements and interventions were generally ignored by the municipality. For the Austrian commission, c a l c undertook to redefine a centre for the village and thereby revitalize its communal life.

c a l c interviewed the village's residents and recorded their aspirations and hopes for the village in words and photographs that delicately express their sense of place, history and community. Many expressed the

**Above** The orange tree in the centre of the village became the symbol of the project.

**Opposite** The completed park in Las Aceñas.

# Now Here: A Park for Las Aceñas

Spain, 1999

wish for a meeting place in the town and their sadness at the village's decline. As a result of the interviews, c a l c decided to work with the village to turn an abandoned, walled plot of land next to the former tannery into a new public space. As part of the community, c a l c were trusted in a way that an incoming group might not have been, demonstrating the value of a sensitive process that uses local agents who have a genuine relationship with and understanding of the local culture.

c a l c decided to use part of their Austrian exhibition budget to buy the land, and hold it in trust as a public park under the villagers' control. The single orange tree left in the abandoned field became the symbol for the project. Photographs of the site were exhibited in the commissioning art space in Linz, and 'orange art' (photographs of the site and other artworks) was sold to finance the project. The representation of their village in the heart of the Linz cultural centre was an important part of the exchange for c a l c.

With the help of some workers from the municipality, the wall was torn down to the height of a bench, the area was cleared and the orange tree freed from thirty years' suffocation by undergrowth. Since the creation of the park, a yearly festival has been hosted which attracts 2,000 people to the tiny village. It now acts as the central communal heart of the village, used informally by the residents to meet, rest and play. Other projects have been initiated as a result; the residents seem to have found the confidence to take action about creating other spaces for the community – a social club and a fishing platform, among others. The elderly retired residents have taken on the responsibility of cleaning and maintaining the park, and have made their own benches and other bits of infrastructure, bypassing the municipal government.

This project shows how a simple, yet much needed, public space intervention can be conceived and managed inventively by creative practitioners, who can engage the community, articulate their desires and use unconventional methods to achieve their aims. The value of the project lies in its simplicity of process and economy of means, appropriate to the location, culture and scale of the community. It is also an interesting case study of using 'art' as a means to achieve political or structural changes that had not been possible through conventional methods, and the role of local creative practitioners as the custodians of the community's needs, articulating them clearly and realizing them creatively.

**Opposite** The artist group interviewed all the residents of the village and gathered their memories and desires for the area.

**Above** The small park lies at the centre of the village but was completely overgrown and unusable. It now hosts a yearly festival.

The Rural Studio, which works in one of the poorest counties of one of the poorest states of the USA, vividly demonstrates the impact of context-based education in a deprived community. It is a pre-eminent model for how an academic institution can work in its hinterland community to produce real change as well as a new model of education.

**Below** The Rural Studio is based in the small town of Newbern, Alabama (population 261).

**Opposite** One of the fifteen homes that have been built by the Rural Studio for local families, experimenting with low-cost materials while aiming to provide decent dwellings.

The Rural Studio was founded in 1993 by the late Samuel Mockbee, a practising architect and teacher from Mississippi. It is an elective design-build architecture studio and part of Auburn University's architecture department, where students investigate, design and construct projects for clients in the deprived 'Black Belt' region, where poverty runs at nearly three times the national rate. The Rural Studio sees its role as educational rather than as social, but defines part of its educational mission as making its students socially engaged citizens. Since 1993 it has built, adapted or repaired over fifty community projects and fifteen houses for families under the poverty line.

The Rural Studio shows that an educational institution can be an effective agent for change in deprived rural areas, where organizations with a high level of capacity are scarce and educated young people tend to leave as soon as they have the opportunity. The benefits are shared between the local community and the students, who become better trained and more employable designers as a result of learning all the parts of the construction process, including physically building the projects. As opposed to traditional forms of educational outreach – classes for the community, research studies on the community, or the use of real places as the sites for hypothetical conjecture – the Rural Studio carries out action research that results in tangible physical and economic change. It proves that academia can use its teaching processes to realize radical change on the ground.

**Opposite** The Antioch Baptist Church, rebuilt by the studio for its tiny congregation who had worshipped on the site for over a century.

**Left** The interior of the church, which reused the timber from the former chapel that had become delapidated and unfit for use.

**Above and right** All the construction work is done by the students, who learn invaluable skills for their later careers in architecture.

**Opposite** A recent project that aimed to build a prototype house that local builders could copy, for a total cost of $20,000 – the limit of a government housing loan programme.

**Above and opposite** The pavilion at Perry Lakes Park is part of ongoing work the Rural Studio has been doing to make this important ecological area more publicly accessible, and to attract more visitors from out of state. This has involved opening in 2006 the highest bird-watching tower in the country. The pavilion, pictured, hosts a programme of events ranging from use as an outdoor classroom, wedding parties and cook outs.

The Rural Studio's projects are acupunctural, targeted at the areas where they can have most impact yet be feasible for the students to undertake. Five projects a year by teams of three to five students range from single-family houses to school buildings, sports facilities, churches and other community buildings. There is an emphasis on experimenting with local materials, innovative technology and low-cost methods of construction which could be used more widely in the area. The projects' timescales are short – between nine months and two years from conception to completion. This also stands in contrast to more traditional academic outreach programmes where a lengthy process of research can take years to have any physical impact. Projects are not always small though – recent examples have included a new firestation for Newbern and a 500-square-metre (5,400-square-foot) Rural Heritage Centre that houses a local food programme and cottage industries outlet. Increasingly, the studio is becoming focused on community projects rather than housing as a way to better meet the economic and social needs of residents.

The Rural Studio's projects have an evolving aesthetic and design identity that reflects both the innovative and unconventional construction techniques and materials that are often used, the emphasis on reuse, reduction of waste and economy, and a deep connection with the Southern vernacular and its landscape that is reinterpreted in contemporary but resonant ways. Its buildings are rooted in a respect for materials and the intimate understanding of detail and craft that the students gain through the hands-on building process, giving the projects a uniquely human quality that the users and community connect with. The materials used – from rammed earth to local timber or catfish netting – reflect the local character and built environment in surprising, imaginative ways, giving value to materials that are often discounted as low-grade and unattractive.

The Rural Studio has been a model for other universities setting up design-build architecture units operating in deprived and rural areas. While urban architecture/planning outreach programmes often operate as an advisory service rather than as a mechanism for delivering physical change, the rural location requires, and allows, a much more active approach and a much deeper connection between the studio and the community. The Rural Studio has been physically and permanently based in the same community

since its inception which has allowed it to become embedded for the long-term as a trusted, integral part of local networks. This is vital to its continued relevance in the area's renewal. The Studio can maintain both an independent profile (not reliant on any local sources of funding) but also a very close relationship with local leaders, officials and non-profit organizations, enabling projects to proceed fast and with the minimum of bureaucracy. The Rural Studio has also been instrumental in setting up a new Housing Resource Center to better serve the housing needs of the area and to act as a pilot programme for other similar centres in other towns.

The Rural Studio model is widely applicable to other areas, institutions and disciplines other than architecture. Using the energy and intellectual capacity of a higher education institution to implement on-the-ground projects both validates the educational process, giving students a skills-set that is relevant to real-world demands, and enables the community to benefit from a more sustainable partnership than short-term grant-funded programmes or voluntary work. The creativity of students and their ambition produces powerful results that go beyond what most conventional agencies would consider possible.

The town of Osuna in southern Spain once had an extensive network of ancient tracks used for the transportation of cattle to nearby hills for pasture. Most of the tracks had been lost or taken over by adjoining agricultural smallholdings and their legal status as public rights of way had been undermined by disputes between farmers. The restoration of these ancient cattle tracks illustrates the delicate nature of rural regeneration.

The tracks had been vital in forming both the character and culture of the area, and became the means by which to engage local communities in the process of regeneration and appreciation of their surroundings. By focusing on the cattle tracks as a single 'object' while approaching them from a

**Right** The cattle tracks are ancient highways that have provided a means of transport and ecological and economic exchange for centuries.

**Opposite** The town of Osuna lies in the centre of Andalucia and its network of ancient paths dates back to Roman times.

# Cattle Tracks
Spain, 1998–2002

multiplicity of angles – ecological, planning, economic, health and leisure – their restoration has been sensitive and holistic, using local understanding combined with expert knowledge. In an area of historic importance but some significant deprivation, the cattle tracks have also been a way to encourage tourism and new activities.

The area around the old town of Osuna, in the heart of Andalucia in southern Spain, has over 400 kilometres (250 miles) of these ancient cattle tracks and drovers' roads which pass through the town and out into the hills. They date from Roman times and were formerly the routes along which cattle were transported between grazing areas or to market. The tracks became important ecological corridors for wildlife exchange as well as sites of historic interest, with ancient natural springs and drinking troughs, as well as footpaths between farms and settlements. They pass through the centre of the town and are linked to the historic planning of the urban fabric.

The neglect of the tracks, or their conscious absorbtion into adjoining smallholdings, undermined their status as public rights of way. The loss of this infrastructure, and the multifunctional role played by the cattle tracks with regard to sustaining the environment in a rural community, led to a series of problems. The genetic exchange among the species of wildlife that used the cattle tracks as ecological corridors was affected; the contact of the public with the environment was limited due to the lack of leisure infrastructure; there was an impact on rural communications because of the lack of a network which would facilitate the appropriate framework for transport and infrastructure; the area's cultural heritage, a large part of which was situated on or nearby the cattle tracks, was inaccessible and deteriorating; and the planning of new urban development did not include any consideration of the tracks' integration.

The municipal council saw the potential to use the cattle tracks restoration as a means to address these issues. Taking a participatory approach, they worked with residents and local groups, including ecologists, ramblers and scouts associations to demarcate and protect nearly all the cattle tracks of Osuna. The process used GIS (Geographical Information System) and historical data mapping to ascertain the exact location of the lost parts of the tracks as well as ground surveys by local groups.

The tracks have been reinstated and signposted, and many of them have been replanted and the old drinking troughs where the ancient natural springs are situated have been restored and rebuilt. Certain tracks are now signed as trails leading to visitor destinations such as lakes for bird-watching and historic sites.

The demarcated cattle tracks have enabled access to the main scientific, cultural and ethnographic areas of interest. The signposting of the cattle tracks and the creation of eco-tourist routes to destinations of particular historic or environmental significance have benefited the local economy and are also used educationally by local schools and training programmes in tourism, environmental studies and archaeology. At the same time, the process raised awareness among the communities about the value of the tracks and the importance of maintaining them as a leisure resource for local people as well as a cultural artefact. The end results are perhaps invisible to the casual visitor, but reveal a sensitivity and distinctiveness that is entirely appropriate for the local context, where a conventional 'regeneration' programme or an over-complex or sweeping approach might destroy the delicate character of the area.

**Opposite** The tracks link the historic centre of the town to remote and varied parts of the rural communities and their landscapes.

# IDENTITY

Snow Culture Project, Japan
OASIS, USA
Invisible Zagreb, Croatia
Common Ground, UK

The identity of a place is made up of many things: the physical environment and lived culture most obviously, but also the broad sweep of heritage, the local values of the community and the symbolic meanings within place. In current conditions, where accelerated development can produce an entirely new suburb or city and small settlements or rural districts can disappear under swathes of new housing, the question of identity becomes critical. Identity can and should be the basis for long-term, successful place-making, a process that nurtures local distinctiveness, pride in place, a culture open to change while respecting continuity with the past.

A process is required that allows for this consideration of identity within planning and practice for renewal – this process might be termed 'characterization'. Characterization has traditionally been seen as a heritage place check – a noting of particular physical or natural features which contribute to an understanding of historic value and identity. A contemporary methodology of characterization, however, that addresses the physical, social and cultural understanding of place, can provide a vital contribution to sustainable urban and rural renewal. This process actively includes the participation of local people and incorporates their values and perceptions of place, mapping the personal and subjective onto the objectivity of a detailed spatial survey.

Local value mapping does not drive a single vision but can enrich the thinking around a multilayered understanding of character and its development. A place may have many different physical and perceptual identities and space should be given for expression of these differences. Characterization can include unexpected results – a community who favour the high-rise block over the terrace, or who prefer the skyline of industry to the majestic river. The dominance of a single vision is replaced by a heterotopian vision, the creation of identity as an ongoing, long-term process which contains a multiplicity of parallel values and understandings, but one that can be clearly articulated, understood and adopted into strategic masterplanning and development.

Mapping is the starting point of characterization – a process of understanding, charting what is there, and developing tools to record and visualize that information. Conventional characterization makes implicit value judgments about the quality of the landscape or built environments, omitting the ordinary or the 'unimportant'. A more inclusive approach to gathering data can reveal qualities and the individual 'fingerprint' of a place that can instigate a much more subtle and imaginative approach to planning, from local value investigation to the gathering of hard data and spatial surveying. In this sense characterization could record anything from biodiversity to the location of landfill

**Opposite** Thurrock: A Visionary Brief demonstrated a new approach to understanding the culture and identity of an area through creative mapping as well as hard data collection in preparation for the setting of masterplanning briefs for wide subregional development.

sites or post offices, or the flight paths of pigeons. New processes for establishing character were developed by General Public Agency's 'Thurrock: A Visionary Brief in the Thames Gateway' which established creative mapping alongside hard data collection to uncover and generate a rich, subtle and accessible resource to aid the strategic planning for regional development. Approaches to regeneration tend to start with economic and infrastructural target setting. Thurrock: A Visionary Brief sought to articulate an alternative approach, developing a process of characterization as the first consideration in a thorough reappraisal of what already exists in an area and therefore what can be used as building blocks for physical, economic and social change. Thurrock: A Visionary Brief was commissioned as a response to central government's plans for Thurrock, a borough that suffers from deprivation and ecological degradation. Situated in the east of London, it is scheduled for major regeneration and new development as part of the 'Thames Gateway' growth area for the south east of England.

The programme involved detailed local research and mapping as the first phase, preparing a comprehensive briefing about all aspects of Thurrock – its economy, landscape, communities, history and culture – the first time that this information had been collated for professional and public use. In addition, artists and writers were commissioned to make their creative response to the area as a way of exploring its often hidden character. Local values and perceptions were investigated through the commissions. Following this mapping and characterization programme, General Public Agency invited twenty international artists, architects, planners and environmentalists to participate in three intensive charrettes (workshops), alongside local authority officers, activists and other local advisers to respond to key challenges facing Thurrock.

The programme demonstrated how, in a short space of time, it is possible to create a visionary yet credible and pragmatic framework for regeneration and raise the profile and aspirations of the area. The project showed how a collaborative, creative process can result in serious, useful and practical thinking for clients. The structure of the programme was centred around the involvement of diverse practitioners at the brief-setting stage rather than as consultants commissioned to fulfil the demands of a brief in which they have little, if any, input. While every regeneration strategy aims to develop an aspirational 'vision', too often the authorities' imagination is hampered by the presence of bureaucratic and closed processes as opposed to a framework that encourages open-ended and distinctive imagination. By embedding radical creative practice into the decision-making and delivery process, and providing decision-makers with new skills and encouragement to think laterally, truly imaginative, innovative and tailor-made solutions become possible.

Mapping is both a way-finding and a political tool and can be used to make comprehensible aspects of land use and planning that are otherwise impenetrable to outsiders. Mapping processes are constantly developing and artists and community activists are producing pioneering work on the potential for such processes to intervene within city use and plans. Public Green was initiated by Lize Mogel, an artist who mapped publicly accessible green space in the city of Los Angeles, which she then displayed on posters throughout the public transport system for two years (see pp. 148–9). The posters could be used to find parks locally or near daily commutes, or as a basis for community advocacy. Cartographic and written information on the poster, in English and Spanish, gave the viewer an understanding of practices of acquisition, creation and maintenance of public green space in relation to Los Angeles economics, real estate practices, and history, thus raising questions about ownership of land, and the transfer of property from private to public use.

Research and mapping processes are integral to a sensitive identification of character and to the support of community-owned identity. Interactive, open-access mapping systems such as that of case study OASIS in New York (see pp. 158–61) demonstrate the potential of mapping as an aid to community planning, action and stewardship. The OASIS project is an exemplar of open-source, accessible hard data that is now a vital tool for both planners and designers who need to make better-informed decisions, and community groups and individuals who want to participate in the planning process or initiate their own projects. OASIS was one of the first web-based mapping resources, and further development of new technologies demonstrates the immense potential for citizen-based characterization. The recent explosion of mapping via web-based open-source mapping frameworks has seen individuals making their own marks on the city, mapping everything from crime statistics to their walks to and from work. Yellow Arrow project and other mobile-phone technologies are starting to add to a rich understanding of the physical landscape that links the perceptual to the physical in ways that planners are only starting to exploit to build up a more detailed understanding of place and value.

In considering identity within planning there is a need to recognize and understand existing identities and also to consider how to support developing identities. The consequent need to accommodate change and development is influencing the parameters of professional practice. Invisible Zagreb – a Squatters' Guide (see pp. 162–7) was a two-year project to map and publicize the potential of the city's empty spaces for use in new forms of social and cultural practice. Invisible Zagreb takes on the vacant, undefined space of the city as material matrix in order to endow the city's spaces with sustainable structures for the future. The project emerged from a city undergoing radical change, where state control and public institutions were increasingly ceding power to private interests. In this context of flux, the initiators of Invisible Zagreb, architect and artist group Platforma 9,81, saw their role change, shifting beyond 'pure discipline'. Instead they seek to operate as 'space managers', champions of the public space and urban planning, engaging the public in the issues of urbanization, regeneration and public space in the city.

Identity is inherently political – ownership of identity can lie within or outside of communities, from large-scale externally focused place-branding programmes to locally owned projects such as Project Row Houses (see pp. 194–9). Place-branding programmes stretch from advertising campaigns targeted at tourists to the branding of Silicon Valley, from the new 'creative quarters' in post-industrial cities to the celebration of small-town quests for distinctiveness, such as 'Catfish Capital of Alabama'.

There is an approach to branding development that proposes that identity be integrated as the driver of economic, spatial and social development plans for an area. Japan has developed this use of identity as a planning tool in a series of revitalization plans using natural features such as snow and star-gazing as the basis of a thorough and integrated approach to development. The Snow Culture Project in the small town of Yasuzuka (see pp. 152–7) demonstrates this inspirational approach to branding and development through planning, by using the intrinsic natural feature of snow to market the area as a tourist destination. This in turn created and supported a successful and diverse economy, increased local skill levels and developed new technologies.

Biseicho, another Japanese rural town in decline, developed a plan for renewal by identifying itself with 'star-gazing'. The implementation of the plan demonstrates the relationship between characterization and architectural, design and landscaping solutions. The plan has resulted in many projects and initiatives, one of which

**Below and opposite** Public Green posters were placed in bus stops all around Los Angeles, putting public space information directly into the public domain. The posters (in two languages) revealed the unseen logic behind the city's planning, describing an aspect of its identity that is not usually considered 'relevant' for public dissemination.

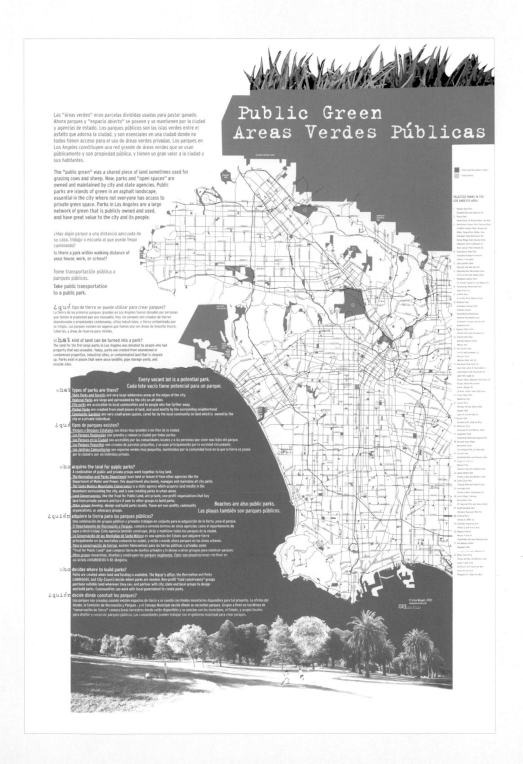

involves designing the physical environment to maximize star-gazing. An ordinance was passed against light pollution, to preserve the best conditions for necessary light for daily life, while keeping the night sky as dark as possible. A two-thirds subsidy was offered for the redesign and rebuilding of facilities to conform to the new law. The light law and related activities in Biseicho have put the town firmly on the star-gazing map in Japan. More than ten thousand visitors come to the town to star-gaze every year now. Most importantly, the sense of civic pride in the town has greatly increased and the decline has been reversed.

Tirana, the capital of Albania, has shifted its identity through a branding programme initiated by the artist mayor Edi Rama, a charismatic figure who coloured the town in vast abstract designs over the façades of sometimes crumbling post-Soviet architecture. This radical facelift is the imposition of one man's vision and has raised controversy both locally and externally but Edi Rama has undoubtedly succeeded in changing the perception of Tirana on a national and international level.

Identity has become a potential tool for architects, landscape designers, artists, planners, government officials and politicians, in the realization that distinctiveness is what people crave, but the process has yet to be embedded. If taken up more widely, however, it would offer an effective route to long-term sustainability and would provide an authenticity that is neither a Disney version of a romanticized local heritage, nor the bland 'anywhere' of low-grade development.

**Left** Part of artist Kerstin Bergendal's programme in Trekroner, Denmark, to build the long-term identity of a major new suburb included commissions such as a bridge by artist Nils Norman that created public space for the emerging community to appropriate and inhabit.

This is not a conservationist vision of distinctiveness and identity – openness always should be there. Places that work happily accommodate a variety of types of people and uses, and are able to weather economic cycles and self-seed and self-regenerate. They do so because they have a strong understanding of the local and inclusivity. It is a question that is increasingly being addressed in new-build developments like that of Trekroner in Denmark where the local authority used Kerstin Bergendal's art plan to inject identity into a new suburb. The approach made space to be appropriated by the incomers – it was not a finished article. Identity will grow over time, but the principles and methods that will allow this growth are there from the outset.

**Above and opposite above** The Plaimont wine-growers cooperative in the southwest of France was trying to revive pride in their unique viticultural identity, traditional varieties and ecological practices which were becoming undermined by mass-market pressures which considered them unsophisticated. In 1993 they brought a living, fruiting vineyard to the main square in Toulouse overnight, with the mayor's consent but without any warning to the public, who woke up to a vintage in progress in the middle of the city and a three-day festival of jazz, theatre, eating and drinking.

**Snow Culture Project in Japan** demonstrates vividly how a creative approach to difficult natural conditions can rebrand and regenerate a rural area. It has built on the local distinctiveness of the town of Yasuzuka to develop not only a new and diverse economy, but also a unique knowledge base of technology and culture in which the town can take pride. If the public identity of a town is to be sustainable and credible it must be based on a place's intrinsic qualities.

In the last half century Yasuzuka has experienced depopulation problems typical of most small towns in Japan. Between 1955 and 1997, its population dropped from 11,000 to 4,300. One of the reasons for this outwards migration was the severe winters it suffers: it experiences snowfall of two to five metres (six to fifteen feet) every year for six months, placing a major burden on the town and its inhabitants.

The catalyst for the Snow Culture Project was the gradual realization that the snow had a value that could be exploited economically. The culture of snow was something that visitors from warmer areas found unique and appealing. This realization of the value that outsiders to the town placed on snow led to the formation of a 'Snow Country Culture Village Plan' by the municipality. This refocused the town's planning on its intrinsic resources – the snow, the countryside around the town and the people of the town. It effectively designated the town

**Above** Snow has become an important part of the town's economy, being 'harvested' for mail-order gifts and commercial use.

**Right** Preparing the packaging for delivery to other parts of the country.

**Opposite** In 1987 the town exported 450 truckloads of snow to Tokyo for a major festival, attracting huge media coverage.

# Snow Culture Project
## Japan, 1986 – ongoing

as a park whose planning had to be led by the need to impact as minimally as possible upon the environment.

In 1986 the town started literally to export snow alongside the speciality food products unique to the area's ecology that they sold by mail order. In 1987 the town transported 450 truckloads of snow, as well as 40 per cent of the town's residents, to Tokyo for a festival – an achievement that attracted huge media coverage. The Snowman Foundation was set up to implement the village plan in 1990. Its holistic and creative mandate has ensured that the town's development has integrated not only economic and spatial planning, but also cultural activities, research, technological innovation and education. The institute was an initiative of the municipality and non-profit organizations, and its management involved participation by schools, the chambers of commerce, cultural and sports associations. Children, women, youth, elderly and other groups run the community centre which was established as a part of the institute.

The Snowman Foundation explores every aspect of snow, from its science and technology to the traditional snow culture of the area, clothing and housing design. It investigates ways of living with and using snow in innovative ways, and this integration of cultural and scientific exploration results in projects that build on traditional knowledge and customs and that address every scale, from town planning to food and drink. The solutions that have resulted from this research have been showcased and applied nationwide, and the town is now a leader in the field. The best-known technological output has been to pioneer the use of stored snow for cooling and air-conditioning. A school and the snow-culture centre were built as models for this technology, which is now used in many other Japanese towns. 'Snow houses' have been built for passive cold food storage linked to the food products that the town makes. Other projects have included new ski-fields and winter sports facilities, hot springs, festivals and competitions.

The Snowman Foundation has also placed a heavy emphasis on education. Children and the women of the town have become involved with ecological education, and the foundation runs courses for local guides, seminars on snow ecology and technology, and graduate courses in environmental studies. It also markets the local products that are grown and made around the town, such as distinctive varieties of rice, soba noodles and

**Top** The area produces unique varieties of rice and other produce that are marketed across the country as 'snow foods'.

**Above** Education projects build awareness among young people of the positive and fascinating aspects of their area.

**Opposite** The Snow Festival and other community events support and celebrate the culture of the area, such as the straw capes traditionally worn by children.

fresh herbs. These can be ordered online or bought at the shop, alongside insulated boxes of the snow itself. The foundation promotes organic and traditional methods of agriculture and trains local farmers in these methods.

Yasuzuka now attracts 100,000 tourists a year and its population has stabilized. Its economy is diverse and sustainable through its research and scientific activities and its agriculture, as well as the eco-tourism and winter sports that it offers, fostering a unique integration of every aspect of the town's life. With the community and its aspirations as the driving force, the town has defined a strong contemporary identity that is genuine and intrinsic to the place, and thus unique.

**Above and opposite** The Snowman Foundation built by architect Jun Aoki in the shape of a snowman demonstrates new technology in action, using stored snow to cool the building in the summer. It provides a meeting space for community activities and training, and hosts conferences and other events.

OASIS – the Open Accessible Space Information System – enables the citizens of New York to characterize and learn about their surroundings, and thus to participate fully in the planning process. It demonstrates the power of new technologies to allow communities to gather and share information in a grassroots way. While GIS – Geographical Information System – has generally been a technology used only by 'professionals', OASIS created an easy-to-use mapping interface combining local authority and federal data, community mapping and academic research findings. Its user-led, participatory design is highly innovative, and its reach and use by citizens who are not technically skilled in new technologies is impressive.

**Opposite** Children and young people add to the store of communal knowledge about the city, which is collected on an open-access web-based database.

OASIS is based on the belief that a common, free, mapping inventory – best hosted on the web – is invaluable to NYC's communities and activists. It enables them not only to learn about their surroundings, but also to use the information to question planning authorities or propose new projects in a fully informed way. OASIS includes data from federal agencies, planning authorities, the census and other 'official' sources, but also from citizen groups such as community gardeners, tree planters, historical societies, birdwatchers and other community groups.

The web service has been designed in collaboration with a grassroots outreach programme (GROW – Grassroots Reassuring OASIS Works) which tested the emerging interface with community groups and other potential users, allowing them to influence the way it was configured. Furthermore, GROW seeks to help local communities identify the resources, technology and information they need to transform their open spaces and brownfield sites, and to incorporate these into the OASIS system.

OASIS works at a high level of detail and is intuitive to use. It includes information on physical features of the city from building use through to ecological status and individual trees, and also data on land ownership and the management organizations of open spaces. It can enable any NYC resident or community group to create customized maps of open space or the built environment by zip code, borough, tax block and lot, and/or neighbourhood. Any individual or group can calculate statistics, locate open-space resources and find them by type or geographic location. It allows

# OASIS
## USA, 2000–ongoing

citizens to undertake 'what if' scenarios, such as modelling the impact of a proposed new development on traffic or the best routes for new cycle paths.

An example of the application of OASIS is the Asthma Free School Zone, which aims to create zones of minimal pollution around schools. Staff from the New York State Attorney General's office have used OASIS to locate areas of the city where bus idling might be a problem. They zoom in on the aerial photos, where concentrations of yellow are visible (indicating a school bus depot), and use maps to identify nearby schools, property owners, and transit routes. This creative way of using online maps to target polluters and nearby impacted schools has played a key role in the Attorney General's office bringing about actions. The settlement that resulted directly benefited the Asthma Free School Zone initiative and communities throughout the city.

OASIS began with twenty-four organizations collaborating and now maintains a network of more than sixty. The website is accessed over 25,000 times each week and people use the OASIS GIS tools to make more than a million maps a year. OASIS allows New Yorkers directly to access the data that planners use to make decisions, as well as to add their own data to the knowledge pool. As such, it powerfully demonstrates the principle of placing high-quality, specialist but accessible research in the public domain, to enable citizens to participate in the decision-making process in an informed way. OASIS represents an exemplary resource and a critical component of the democratization of the planning system.

**Opposite and above** Detailed maps of the city can be created by users and also specifically for the needs of community groups and municipal authorities. This information is readily available to all via the website.

**Classified Land Cover**
**Northern Staten Island - Community Board 1**

Legend
Classified Land Cover

- Unknown
- Tree/Shrub
- Grass
- Other Impervious Land
- Buildings
- Water
- Water

Color infrared images collected by the EMERGE Corporation were taken in September, 2001. Each pixel in the image was classified as either tree/shrub (dark green), grass/soil (light green), buildings (grey), other impervious land (tan), and water (blue). Classification accuracy on Staten Island is 74%.
Source: USDA Forest Service, Northeastern Research Station
Aerial photos taken September, 2001

0    0.5    1 Miles

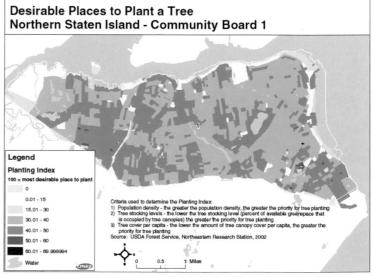

**Desirable Places to Plant a Tree**
**Northern Staten Island - Community Board 1**

Legend
Planting Index
100 = most desirable place to plant

- 0
- 0.01 - 15
- 15.01 - 30
- 30.01 - 40
- 40.01 - 50
- 50.01 - 60
- 60.01 - 69.999994
- Water

Criteria used to determine the Planting Index:
1) Population density - the greater the population density, the greater the priority for tree planting
2) Tree stocking levels - the lower the tree stocking level (percent of available greenspace that is occupied by tree canopies) the greater the priority for tree planting
3) Tree cover per capita - the lower the amount of tree canopy cover per capita, the greater the priority for tree planting
Source: USDA Forest Service, Northeastern Research Station, 2002

0    0.5    1 Miles

# Value of the Neighborhood Trees Surveyed
# Northern Staten Island - Community Board 1

The total value of the 212 trees on Staten Island was $975,969.00 (all = $1,038,458.00) with a mean value of $4,603.63 (all = $3,225.03). The total amount of carbon sequestration* conducted by the 212 trees on Staten Island is 4,005.14 kg/year with a mean value of 18.89 kg/year. Table describes the 5 most valuable trees surveyed on Staten Island.

| Common Name | Scientific Name | Age (yrs) | Tree Condition | Compensatory Value ($) | Carbon Sequestration (kg/year)* |
|---|---|---|---|---|---|
| Tuliptree | Liriodendron tulipifera | 214 | Excellent | 23069.00 | 62.26 |
| London Plane | Platanus x acerifolia | 200 | Good | 22109.00 | 13.87 |
| Pin Oak | Quercus palustris | 125 | Good | 18156.00 | 48.95 |
| European beech | Fagus sylvatica | 234 | Good | 17207.00 | 50.98 |
| Tuliptree | Liriodendron tulipifera | 126 | Excellent | 17053.00 | 43.88 |

*carbon sequestration = carbon capture, separation, and storage or reuse.
Source: TreesNY and CENYC, Citizen Pruners, and USDA Forest Service, Northeastern Research Station, 2002

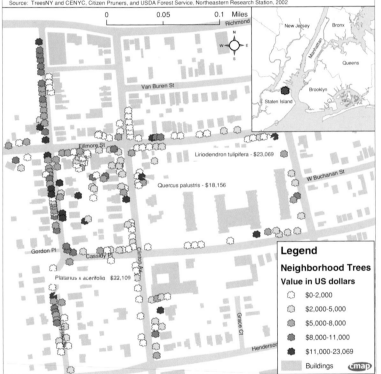

## Legend
**Neighborhood Trees**
**Value in US dollars**
- $0-2,000
- $2,000-5,000
- $5,000-8,000
- $8,000-11,000
- $11,000-23,069
- Buildings

# Neighborhood Trees Surveyed
# Northern Staten Island - Community Board 1

212 neighborhood trees were surveyed in the New Brighton/Livingston neighborhood of Staten Island. All of the trees are located in Community Board 1. Of the trees surveyed, 18 were in excellent condition, 176 in good condition, and 18 in poor condition. 64 of the trees are London plane tree (Platanus x acerifolia), 30 are Norway maple (Acer platanoides), and 11 are Silver maple (Acer saccharinum). The most valuable tree surveyed is an estimated 214 year old Tuliptree or Yellow-poplar (Liriodendron tulipifera) in excellent condition valued at $23,069.00. The 2nd and 3rd most valuable trees are a 200 year old London plane tree (Platanus x acerifolia) and a 125 year old Pin oak (Quercus palustris) valued at $22,109.00 and $18,156.00 respectively and both in good condition.

Source: TreesNY and CENYC, Citizen Pruners, and USDA Forest Service, Northeastern Research Station, 2002

## Legend
- Neighborhood Trees
- Buildings
- Water

Invisible Zagreb was a two-year project by Platforma 9,81 to investigate and showcase the potential of the city's empty spaces for emergent forms of social practices and developments in the future. It provides an alternative methodology for planning in a city undergoing fast and profound change. In the post-transitional context of rapid privatization and deregulation, it has created a simple strategy to influence the actual, real use of urban space and buildings, the political agenda and the engagement of the wider public with issues of urban space and buildings, without an overtly 'educational' or 'activist' framework.

**Opposite** A disused mill in the centre of Zagreb, one of the many empty spaces mapped by the Invisible Zagreb project.

Croatia, like many other countries in the region, has been undergoing a process of political and economic reform that traditional urban planning struggles to keep up with. In the hiatus of control over the city's development, issues of identity, public realm and heritage have become sidelined through the lack of cooperation between state and private sector agents. These issues are common not only to Eastern Europe but to other fast-developing countries where economic liberalization is occurring alongside a vacuum in the governmental capacity to regulate. On an urban scale, Zagreb has experienced a lack of leadership in planning, and massive growth of private development without an infrastructural or public programme to support this.

The aim of Invisible Zagreb was to investigate the 'holes' in the city's proprietary and physical matrix – the buildings and spaces that had been abandoned and largely forgotten about as development occured around them, due to ambiguities over ownership and the relative difficulty of negotiating the reuse of existing buildings. By mapping these spaces and encouraging new temporary uses of them, a parallel strategy for the creation of a public realm was created and continues to influence the formation of policy and practice in the city. The project investigates the possibilities of informal urban and cultural strategies that can inhabit these spaces with temporary public activity and serve as a strategic delay before the ultimate changes take place.

The central focus of the project was to map all the major empty spaces in Zagreb, ranging from factories to abandoned cinemas, hospitals and stations. Each space was mapped onto a data sheet that recorded information including size, floorplans and sections, ownership, and condition of repair

# Invisible Zagreb
Croatia, 2003–2005

alongside photos and drawings. Through this categorization, the potential for reuse of each structure could be revealed and the placing of this information in the public domain encouraged other groups to make use of the spaces, with technical assistance from the Invisible Zagreb team.

The next stage was to organize temporary events in the spaces, ranging from music festivals attracting 3,000 people, to art installations, film screenings and tours, putting these forgotten spaces on the mental map of the city and raising their profile with both the public and the city authorities. These projects acted as test cases to investigate the feasibility of potential new functions in the spaces, and involved the public directly rather than through contrived methods of 'participation'.

Active media coverage of the events has enabled Invisible Zagreb to become part of a city-wide debate about the future of these spaces. The last part of the project is to record and collate the activities that have happened as a way to suggest potential permanent uses for the spaces for commerce, leisure, or cultural facilities. This 'bottom-up planning' is seen both as a tool and a final result of collaboration between city departments and other groups working in urban and cultural policy issues. Through initiating and researching the project, relationships were formed between the professions, the political, public and

private sectors, and the general public, and the collaboration of these partners became the opportunity to develop new urban strategies.

Invisible Zagreb has tested the viability of a different means of planning for cultural and public uses – a blending of an organizational, cartographic approach with the flat networks of cultural groups, informal micro-economies and a do-it-yourself attitude. It has used action research to explore the possibility of harnessing 'marginal' or ambiguous activities as a way of generating more long-term plans for public and social spaces that can become accepted parts of an official urban plan. The project led to an increasing involvement with the city's planning processes, including the planning of cultural and public uses in new development areas.

**Above and opposite** The buildings were photographed, documented and mapped to form an interactive survey that could be used to plan events and new uses. The buildings included abandoned industrial structures (above left), hospitals (above) and cinemas and office blocks (opposite).

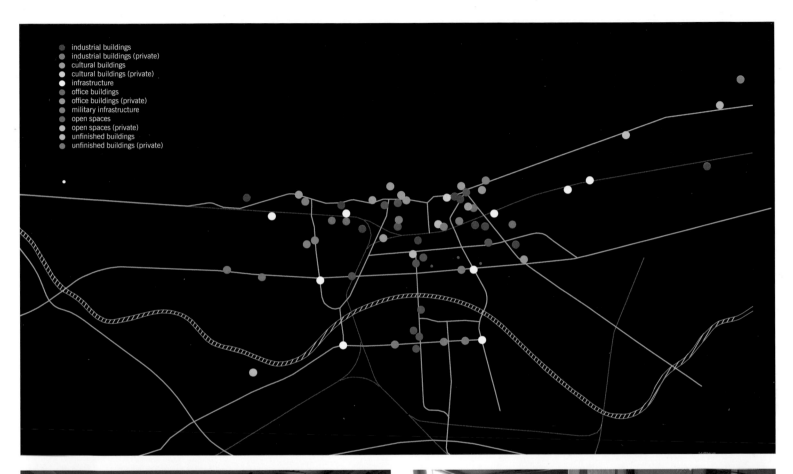

- industrial buildings
- industrial buildings (private)
- cultural buildings
- cultural buildings (private)
- infrastructure
- office buildings
- office buildings (private)
- military infrastructure
- open spaces
- open spaces (private)
- unfinished buildings
- unfinished buildings (private)

**Above and right** Events, from art installations to talks and music festivals, demonstrated the potential uses of the 'holes' in the urban fabric.

**Opposite** *Red Empty*, an installation by artist Carl Michael von Hauswolff in a former liquor factory, was seen by over 25,000 people.

township communities and home to 250,000 people. As a result of the protests, the council asked the communities to join a development forum to contribute ideas about how they would like to see the area developed and the Ecocity concept was born. Ecocity wanted to create a physical demonstration of an environmentally and socially sustainable alternative development path. Since poverty was the major cause of the problems, job creation through 'ecological' industries such as recycling, organic farming and green energy technologies, among others, was seen as an important start. The community unanimously supported all the eco-technologies such as solar, water recycling and passive thermal design. The urban eco-village strategy came into place as a way of exemplifying how sustainable, holistic development could be delivered from first principles.

The Ivory Park slum was characterized by the poor living conditions, unemployment and ecologically unsustainable development patterns that are common to hundreds of communities in the Johannesburg metropolis. Ecocity embraced integrated planning at every level, closely examining the social, physical, natural and economic context through a *State of the Environment* report that provided the detailed baseline characterization of poverty, housing, resource use, pollution and consumption patterns against which future change could be measured. From the beginning Ecocity was set up to be owned and run by the community, leading to often difficult decision-making processes and prioritizing education and capacity building to enable the community to make informed decisions about the planning of the area.

The Ecocity programme now comprises a series of cooperatives that undertake different business activities, based in and around the physical hub of a demonstration eco-village, community centre and market. The cooperatives grow and sell food, recycle, repair bicycles, build environmentally designed homes, fabricate and promote green energy solutions, and work as eco-tourism guides. The food cooperative contains over seventy farmers and in total more than three hundred jobs have been directly created through these cooperatives, in addition to the many hundreds more people who have taken part in the training programmes that have given them a new livelihood. The use of cooperatives as the institutions of choice has proven to be an important factor in the success of the projects, enabling the local people to feel that they have control over their decisions and it has strengthened democracy.

**Above** One of the entrances to Ivory Park Ecocity.

**Opposite** The Ecocity has developed and tested new building techniques for cheap, sustainable homes, and trained local residents in the skills necessary, while also showcasing more 'traditional' building types.

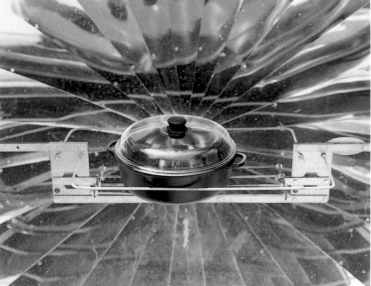

The central part of Ecocity has been the building of the physical eco-village and other buildings, demonstrating in practice new technologies and materials (such as building blocks made from recycled polystyrene). The design and engineering for the buildings was provided by the multinational engineering and architecture firm Arup, combining their technical expertise with the materials and processes already available in the area, and the process was highly participatory in accordance with Ecocity's guiding principles. To train local people in marketable skills that led to the formation of the building cooperative, Arup's local office held weekly workshops in construction skills for the community. Women and youths are now trained in intensive courses at the partner organization Wildrocke before using their skills in the community. The development runs on permaculture principles and harvests rainwater, recycles all grey water, includes green roofs, uses solar energy or low-smoke biomass for energy, and recycles materials as an enterprise.

The impact of Ecocity has been felt on a local, national and continental scale. Locally, the education and training programmes have resulted in a community that is approaching sustainability in their capacity to continue changing their environment and living conditions. Nationally, Ecocity has initiated a unique partnership between several government departments and programmes to train youth in sustainable construction skills, which enables them to get an accredited qualification within a year while helping to solve South Africa's shortfall of 2.3 million homes. Previously many of the programmes aiming to meet this backlog resulted in poor construction quality as a result of a lack of skills. On a wider scale, Ecocity is now working with Bioregional to develop further eco-villages and mixed developments, using their local roots to 'Africanize' zero-carbon principles so that they are appropriate for the local culture and climate.

**Left** Solar cookers developed by Matthias Weber use no fuel or electricity. They are mounted on bicycles for mobility. Previous oil drum cookers created high levels of pollution and dependency on cutting down trees for fuel.

**Opposite** The Ecocity works on a cooperative model, with participants responsible for their own management and development supported by the Ecocity programme.

Common Ground create and champion tools for others to use through a series of pioneering programmes. Their understanding of the everyday and the ordinary as the foundation of the delicate character of places is radical yet pragmatic, reinvigorating not only a cultural and economic sensitivity in place-making, but also an economic argument linking rural communities to the land. Common Ground's approach to revealing, enabling and supporting local distinctiveness crucially recognizes the importance of a long-term approach.

**Above** 'Apple Day' is one of Common Ground's best-known innovations. Now a national event, it created a means for local communities to discover and celebrate the traditional orchards which are often unnoticed and destroyed.

**Opposite** The Common Ground programme provides advice and support for groups who wish to protect and publicize their hidden orchards and has been responsible for the renaissance of local apple varieties.

Common Ground is a charity based in Shaftesbury, Dorset, set up in 1982. Their work is founded on the belief that our relationship with the environment is key to protecting it. It is driven by the importance of understanding place in an intimate and specific way. The organization seeks to inspire people to engage with the richness of everyday places, popular culture, common wildlife, ordinary buildings and landscapes, using celebration as a starting point for action. They offer ideas, information and inspiration for communities to become actively involved in caring for and contributing to their environment but also contribute to policy and programmes internationally.

Common Ground's community orchards programme sees orchards as embodiments of nature, culture and place, and repositories of local distinctiveness. Orchards were once widespread throughout the UK, planted with local varieties of fruit and part of a sustainable, cyclical economy, but pressure on land for new houses and roads and the availability of cheap fruit from abroad has resulted in the loss of 64 per cent in area of orchards in thirty years. Those in villages and on the edges of towns are prime targets for development. Since 1990 the Community Orchards programme has promoted ways to save vulnerable old orchards as well as to plant new ones.

Orchards are seen by Common Ground as a kernel for wider social renewal. Orchards are now being maintained in cities, towns or villages, near housing estates, industrial estates, hospitals and schools. Some pay for themselves with income from the sale of fruit and other products from wildflower seeds to mistletoe, or by being used as campsites or for horticultural or conservation training. The community orchards are promoted as places for festive gatherings, play, contemplation, wildlife watching,

# Common Ground
UK, 1982–ongoing

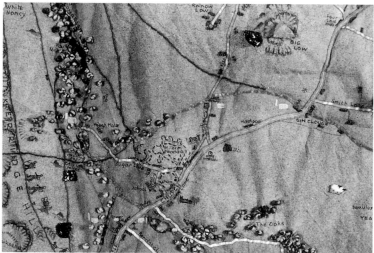

**Above and opposite** Details of contrasting Parish Maps, created by villages to communicate their unique landscapes and cultures. Their handmade nature makes visible the character and personal associations of an area, qualities that are not caught in 'official' planning processes.

animal grazing, skill sharing, building responsibility, nurturing biodiversity, keeping and extending local apple varieties and championing local identity. An additional initiative, Tree Dressing Day, was initiated by Common Ground in 1990. This aims to encourage the celebration of trees in city and country, in the street or village green to highlight our responsibility for looking after trees and reminds us of their cultural and environmental importance.

Common Ground also developed the process of Parish Mapping – an exercise in mapping local features, communal and personal knowledge, and sites of perhaps unrecognized importance in rural parishes, that has since been used in communities all over Britain and as far away as Lithuania and British Columbia. The aim of a Parish Map is to demonstrate what people claim as their own locality and what they value in it: wildlife, history, work, landmarks, buildings, people, festivals. It does not have to be precise or cartographically correct, but by illustrating locally distinctive activities and features, focuses on the everyday things that make a place significant and different from the next. It can include the elusive responses which cannot be measured or counted and also the invisible, the stories, dialect, names and fragments of everyone's history.

As Sue Clifford, co-founder of Common Ground, states: 'The question "What do you value in your place?" turns everyone into experts'. Parish Maps are intended as a starting point for local action: demonstrative, subjective statements made by and for a community, exploring and showing what it cares about in its locality and reversing the usual expert/layperson paradigm. They offer a way of communicating creatively and socially how rich everyday places are, and what importance seemingly ordinary things have to everyone. All kinds of people old and young, from varied cultural backgrounds, by sharing their ideas and knowledge begin to cherish their locality and often become involved directly in its care. 'Parish' is offered not to define but to describe the scale at which people feel a sense of familiarity and ownership in their place: familiar territory, the locality which 'belongs' to you. Other Common Ground projects, such as New Milestones (making new landmarks in villages in Dorset), Confluence (celebrating the river Stour), Field Days and Flora Britannica, all share these deeply held values and also contribute vitally to a body of knowledge about the English countryside.

All of Common Ground's projects promote a unique appreciation of the power of local identity and character in making culturally rich, inclusive local communities. Their encyclopedic approach is evident in their book *England in Particular*. Their process of independent research, dissemination, high-profile and determined campaigning and support for grassroots local communities, demonstrates the power of individual activism and a strong, independent voice. The rigour and determination with which Common Ground champions local characteristics that are unseen by the 'authoritative' voices of planning and heritage exemplify the inclusive attitude towards culture and communities that are shared by all the projects in this book.

# URBAN

Mobile City Farm, USA
Ivory Park Ecocity, South Africa
Project Row Houses, USA
Elemental, Chile
Play or Rewind, Italy

Exploding, shrinking, swelled by migration and suffering environmental destruction, cities always have been and always will be in a state of flux. Change is the key experience of urbanism and all the projects shown in this chapter address how change can be managed as a key element in a process. Yet within the character of urban life there is energy and surprise, lateral exploitation of resources, great civic acts, quiet contemplation, different perspectives, great contrasts. For a truly radical and effective new approach to urban change, we must acknowledge that the issues of how we experience, plan and design cities is more complex, more challenging and more interesting than many practitioners have previously perceived.

The projects in this section present a radically different approach to urbanism. Whether they are constructing masterplans and renewal strategies (as in Ivory Park Ecocity or Project Row Houses), or presenting programmes that act as a challenge, mirror or complement to existing urban initiatives (such as De Strip), they are characterful and visionary. Individuals and groups have found ways to engage city communities and the many other players involved in urban development in fruitful, long-term partnerships that do not compromise creativity and vision for being inclusive. Each is unique to its physical and social space, taking context seriously and finding creative and inventive responses to local conditions.

The projects showcased fully engage with the concept of change as an ongoing process within which specific projects can only play one part. These projects do not treat the process of development or renewal as reaching a fixed end-point where regeneration is achieved but are long-term in their aspirations, allowing for cumulative change punctuated with discrete projects. This approach to the cyclical reuse of city space is most evident in the case study Mobile City Farm (pp. 182–5) which creates temporary agriculture on vacant plots around the city of Chicago in a pragmatic and wholly sustainable relationship with the city authorities. While writing this essay, we stumbled upon the following wonderful quote about its precursor in Philadelphia 100 years ago. Published in 1906 in the UK's commercial property industry magazine, *Estates Gazette*, an editorial entitled 'Not Waste Lands' commented: 'the country has been mildly amused by the unemployed "land grabbers" who have seized waste land in London and a provincial city and begun to plant vegetables upon them. It is difficult not to sympathize with their object of growing food upon soil which at present produces nothing. In the US city of Philadelphia there exists a Vacant Lots Association, where unused building land is handed over to the very poor for growing vegetables until it is otherwise required. Could not this example be followed here?'

Temporary projects can be important ways of shifting perceptions, testing and suggesting new directions in a more lighthearted or provocative way. This is demonstrated by the case study Play and Rewind (see pp. 204–209) and City Joker (p. 176), where for 72 hours two architects travelled along an arbitrarily drawn line through the city, crossing buildings, canals, church roofs and walls. When the line crossed actual homes they conducted interviews with people and produced postcards portraying the inner feelings of the inhabitants, which were then sent along the line. The houses along the line became a new neighbourhood whose inhabitants proudly referred to themselves as 'line people'. One of the participants, Fritz Ostermayr, said on radio: 'it was a day, as blissful as it can be, one of those very rare days. We have "re-discovered" public space – a city vivid as it can be.' Limite Limite, a project by City Mine(d) in Brussels, or some of the activities organized by Marco Casagrande and GAPP in Taiwan, have a similar quality, between festival and political rally, that enriches urban life and provokes open-ended debate about urban futures.

De Strip is a particularly important project in the way that it, and the long-term commissioning programme that it was part of (Until We Meet Again), provided a vital counterpart to a sweeping regeneration process that threatened the unity of a fragile and deprived community. Through the way it reappropriated one of the condemned

Limite Limite, in Brussels, was a temporary 'beacon' used as an exhibition and meeting space. It became a catalyst for linking together different groups in the area, from banks to schools and residents' groups.

buildings, and through the programme of events and activities that it housed, it provided the only link between the past and the present, playing an enormously important role in allowing the community to share the experience of such massive change.

De Strip also highlights the importance of integrity and quality. It is an easily replicable strategy, but if reproduced in a way that was merely an effort to placate or avoid confrontation, not only would it no longer engage the community in any meaningful way, but it would also run the risk of causing much greater alienation and destruction of the local culture. This warning touches on the vitally important consideration of ethics in planning, and the duty of care towards communities whose capacity may be limited and who may require advocacy.

The recognition of value in so-called 'ordinary' or forgotten parts of the city, and the importance of allowing urban spaces to remain rich in possibility rather than deterministic, reaches its most radical expression in works such as artist Lara Almarcegui's Dock Wasteland, a commentary on the insatiable appetite for land and urban development on brownfield 'derelict' sites. Her project used a commission for a piece of public art in the rapidly redeveloping Rotterdam docklands to buy the piece of land, which had spectacular waterfront views, and ensure its designation as open

wasteland for the foreseeable future. It was both a commentary on the unrecognized ecological richness of brownfield sites (where certain species of flora and fauna grow exclusively) and on the importance of empty 'free' space to accommodate future dreams. 'What made the terrain so interesting, was how open it was to any possibility; I decided that my project would consist of leaving the piece of ground…not defined so everything happens by chance and not corresponding to a determined plan. Therefore, nature develops its own way and interrelates with the spontaneous use given to the land and with other external factors like wind, rain, sun and flora. Wastelands are important because one can only feel free in this type of land, forgotten by town planners. I imagine that, in a few years, this will be the only empty land once the surrounding lands are built on.'

**Above** Lara Almarcegui's Dock Wasteland, a publicly accessible piece of undeveloped land in Rotterdam that is preserved specifically as a wasteland.

**Opposite** City Joker drew an arbitrary line through Graz along which two architects travelled by any means necessary, creating a new community and perspective on the city.

Many of these projects, whether short- or long-term, act as mirrors or counterparts to conventional development processes, appropriating some of the conceptual and physical space to create room for communal expression, visions and the creation of new identities from the ground up. WiMBY! (Welcome into My Back Yard!) – whose name is a play on the traditional notion of Nimby (not in my back yard) attitudes – addressed precisely this territory: the creation of identity during the massive regeneration of a 'failed' new town in the Netherlands. The initiative was devised as a ten-year programme of educational projects, festivals, built projects and temporary installations for existing residents and incoming inhabitants, repositioning the town as a desirable and exciting place to live. WiMBY! views rapid social and cultural change as an opportunity for enriching cultural and social infrastructure rather than as a force to be resisted. The programme aims to capitalize on the social, physical and economic assets of the location: from the vast construction of new residential areas, motorway networks, new metro line and light railway to its large numbers of young people from different ethnic backgrounds who use schools, discos, sports fields and music studios.

The restoration of the dilapidated Hotel Prince George in Manhattan, New York, to house key-workers (such as nurses and police) and the homeless side by side, with a

**Above** One of the projects by WiMBY! in Vlaardingen, which engaged new and old residents in sharing and meeting one another through a cumulative programme exploring local values and imaging the future.

**Opposite** The lobby of the Hotel Prince George, now restored to its former glory and housing homeless people and key-workers in equal parts.

holistic programme of services and activities, has created a unique integrated community. It is a demonstration of the inversion of conventional value systems not dissimilar to the communist Mayor of Bologna's policy in the 1980s to turn the grand but vacant city centre historical building, Palazzo Bentivoglio, into social housing thereby invigorating the urban core. In New York, Hotel Prince George has served as a focus for neighbourhood regeneration, with a 28 per cent rise in local property values and a 60 per cent fall in the crime rate since the project started in 1997. The Prince George descended from an exclusive Beaux-Arts hotel to one of the most crime ridden of New York's welfare hotels, housing 1,700 adults and children in nightmare conditions. It was finally condemned and closed down in 1990. In 1997 the NY-based housing and homelessness charity Common Ground purchased the abandoned hotel and restored it to its former splendour. It lets the 416 studio apartments to equal numbers of single key-workers and formerly homeless people. The security of being able to live in a clean, secure, affordable and community-oriented environment has vastly improved the quality of life of its residents. Mixed resident placement in the building (key workers and the homeless living side by side) fosters tolerance and the opportunity for supporting individuals. Residents are welcome to stay as long as they like, even though incomes typically increase from $14,000 to $25,000 once they have the stability of permanent and affordable accommodation. Recently, the huge Ballroom has also been restored to its former lustre. Working with the Parsons School of Architecture, YouthBuild USA and the Brooklyn High School of the Arts,

the Ballroom Restoration Campaign offered young people training and apprenticeships in design, construction and historic restoration. Common Ground's tenants, as well as tenants of other supportive housing, benefit from the jobs created to manage and operate the Ballroom.

One of the key themes emerging from the field of practice described in this book is how to encourage and mediate between the multiple possible readings of a city, rather than conventional visions that only can produce monocultural 'solutions'. The emphasis on building an understanding of what is already there – a characterization – tends not to be used, and is often not considered at all in urban strategies or urbanism as practised. A dry, monocultural, ultimately private and corporate vision is stretching from international airports to urban districts in Dubai or Seoul with little attempt to integrate time and space, environment and culture.

The characters of cities are made up of contrasts, of varied densities, of conflicting uses side by side, weathering fast-paced change, and more subtle heterogeneous states. Development or regeneration in cities never starts from a blank slate, yet an emphasis on

building on existing character and culture, except in the most superficial historicist way, is rarely present in urban development.

Urban areas need to keep their unique character and identity without losing the possibility for change and shifts in perception – a marrying of the past and the future that is arguably about making less rules, not more. The principles of 'New Urbanism' that were intended to combat the sterility of corporate architecture, have merely resulted in a new version of the same; a set of rules that are too often applied unthinkingly to every situation without regard to a site's unique character.

The genuine (as opposed to the contrived, the fake, the sanitized) and how one seeks that out; leaving the space (physical and conceptual) for uncertainty and spontaneity, the unplanned: these ideas are challenging the authority of any one body to determine all future possibilities and rule out the unforeseen, the potentially dangerous and the controversial.

The backdrop is the speed of urban development around the globe, which over recent years is almost impossible to conceive. In 1950 there were two mega-cities (London and New York): in 2005 there were twenty-eight. By the year 2050 it is estimated that the total world population will reach ten billion and two thirds will be living in urban environments. Our global populations are becoming more and more urban. In this context of accelerated development new lessons are coming from unexpected sources and with them, slowly but noticeably, planners, policymakers and developers are beginning to recognize the breadth of what urban life constitutes, and to reflect this in practice. The more fundamental shift, however, is in recognizing that responsibility for, and delivery of, renewal requires active citizenship and a new reading of who the agents of change are.

**Opposite** Treasure Hill in Taipei, a former squatters' colony, became a site of artist and activist projects after it was threatened with destruction. The subsequent designation of the area as a 'cultural quarter' has been controversial with surrounding residents. This project illustrates the difficulty and complexities of competing perspectives.

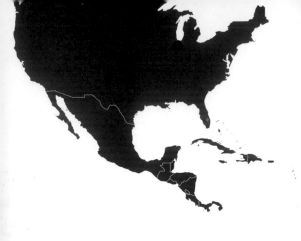

The Mobile City Farm presents an exemplary process for using vacant sites in the city during the inevitable urban cycle of demolition and development. It contributes to an intensive and efficient use of urban land by ensuring that a site can be used productively even while 'derelict' or awaiting construction. It also demonstrates how temporary projects can benefit the city both economically and socially, raising land values while providing the city with much-needed resources – in this case, green space, healthy food and job opportunities.

**Opposite** Mobile City Farm is an unexpected sight in a highly deprived part of Chicago. At the time that this photo was taken, in 2005, it was located in a large plot near the infamous Cabrini Green estate.

The Mobile City Farm is a project created by Resource Center Chicago, a non-profit organization that works with recycling of waste, education and job training. With an estimated 80,000 vacant city lots in Chicago, mostly in economically underdeveloped neighbourhoods, turning vacant land into an asset for the community is its main objective. It has developed a strategy for setting up a working, commercial organic farm on any vacant lot in the city. The City Farm offers more than city beautification and provision of public green space; by producing a significant amount of organic produce that is sold to local residents, many of whom have little or no access to cheap, nutritious food, it also provides job training and employment.

The process of transforming a site into a city farm begins by clearing it and putting down a protective clay barrier to prevent leaching from any toxic materials left behind. Then fresh soil is brought in which is fertilized organically with compost generated from restaurant waste and grass clippings that would normally go into landfill. The final step is to invite unemployed and homeless people to learn about organic farming and apply for apprenticeships on these sites. The project's aim is to educate homeless people and provide them with support so that, within two years, they are knowledgeable enough to care for a farm independently. Having the area occupied and productive makes it more appealing to prospective real-estate developers. When the site is sold, the group literally rolls up the compost and fencing and relocates, leaving a perfectly clean site, ready for redevelopment.

The farm sells its produce to the public from an on-site market stand at lower-than-market prices, making healthy produce available to low-income families. The produce grown at City Farm is also sold at higher prices to

# Mobile City Farm
## USA, 1999 – ongoing

Ivory Park Ecocity is a physical demonstration of environmentally and socially sustainable urban development, combining local expertise with international innovation in an incremental way. It takes a holistic approach to eco-development as a vehicle to reduce poverty and increase the community's capacity to help itself, and is based on the understanding that poverty is exacerbated by modern solutions that require large-scale infrastructure and the use of non-renewable resources. As a major initiative involving government agencies, NGOs, large design firms and developers, it shows how independent activist projects can partner with institutional organizations to enable large-scale realization without losing their ethos and integrity.

The Ecocity project was started by a group of environmentalists and social activists who joined together to protest against council plans to build a toxic dump next to Ivory Park, one of Greater Johannesburg's most deprived

**Left** One of the new community buildings at Ecocity, with garden plots in the background. Ivory Park has tested a number of new building techniques for wider application.

**Opposite** Ivory Park is one of the largest townships in the wider Johannesburg region, home to a quarter of a million people.

# Ivory Park Ecocity
## South Africa, 1993–ongoing

township communities and home to 250,000 people. As a result of the protests, the council asked the communities to join a development forum to contribute ideas about how they would like to see the area developed and the Ecocity concept was born. Ecocity wanted to create a physical demonstration of an environmentally and socially sustainable alternative development path. Since poverty was the major cause of the problems, job creation through 'ecological' industries such as recycling, organic farming and green energy technologies, among others, was seen as an important start. The community unanimously supported all the eco-technologies such as solar, water recycling and passive thermal design. The urban eco-village strategy came into place as a way of exemplifying how sustainable, holistic development could be delivered from first principles.

The Ivory Park slum was characterized by the poor living conditions, unemployment and ecologically unsustainable development patterns that are common to hundreds of communities in the Johannesburg metropolis. Ecocity embraced integrated planning at every level, closely examining the social, physical, natural and economic context through a *State of the Environment* report that provided the detailed baseline characterization of poverty, housing, resource use, pollution and consumption patterns against which future change could be measured. From the beginning Ecocity was set up to be owned and run by the community, leading to often difficult decision-making processes and prioritizing education and capacity building to enable the community to make informed decisions about the planning of the area.

The Ecocity programme now comprises a series of cooperatives that undertake different business activities, based in and around the physical hub of a demonstration eco-village, community centre and market. The cooperatives grow and sell food, recycle, repair bicycles, build environmentally designed homes, fabricate and promote green energy solutions, and work as eco-tourism guides. The food cooperative contains over seventy farmers and in total more than three hundred jobs have been directly created through these cooperatives, in addition to the many hundreds more people who have taken part in the training programmes that have given them a new livelihood. The use of cooperatives as the institutions of choice has proven to be an important factor in the success of the projects, enabling the local people to feel that they have control over their decisions and it has strengthened democracy.

**Above** One of the entrances to Ivory Park Ecocity.

**Opposite** The Ecocity has developed and tested new building techniques for cheap, sustainable homes, and trained local residents in the skills necessary, while also showcasing more 'traditional' building types.

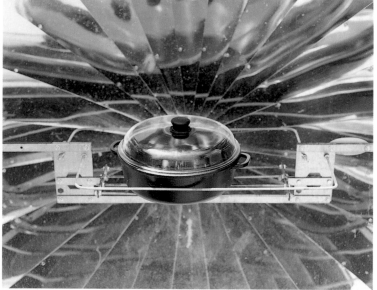

The central part of Ecocity has been the building of the physical eco-village and other buildings, demonstrating in practice new technologies and materials (such as building blocks made from recycled polystyrene). The design and engineering for the buildings was provided by the multinational engineering and architecture firm Arup, combining their technical expertise with the materials and processes already available in the area, and the process was highly participatory in accordance with Ecocity's guiding principles. To train local people in marketable skills that led to the formation of the building cooperative, Arup's local office held weekly workshops in construction skills for the community. Women and youths are now trained in intensive courses at the partner organization Wildrocke before using their skills in the community. The development runs on permaculture principles and harvests rainwater, recycles all grey water, includes green roofs, uses solar energy or low-smoke biomass for energy, and recycles materials as an enterprise.

The impact of Ecocity has been felt on a local, national and continental scale. Locally, the education and training programmes have resulted in a community that is approaching sustainability in their capacity to continue changing their environment and living conditions. Nationally, Ecocity has initiated a unique partnership between several government departments and programmes to train youth in sustainable construction skills, which enables them to get an accredited qualification within a year while helping to solve South Africa's shortfall of 2.3 million homes. Previously many of the programmes aiming to meet this backlog resulted in poor construction quality as a result of a lack of skills. On a wider scale, Ecocity is now working with Bioregional to develop further eco-villages and mixed developments, using their local roots to 'Africanize' zero-carbon principles so that they are appropriate for the local culture and climate.

**Left** Solar cookers developed by Matthias Weber use no fuel or electricity. They are mounted on bicycles for mobility. Previous oil drum cookers created high levels of pollution and dependency on cutting down trees for fuel.

**Opposite** The Ecocity works on a cooperative model, with participants responsible for their own management and development supported by the Ecocity programme.

While Ecocity is a South African solution to local problems, its approach to community renewal and lifting communities out of cyclical deprivation holds lessons for Western cities. The emphasis on building an ethic of local involvement and ownership and a community that holds the capacity to initiate and continue changing itself is strong. This long-term scenario is not about 'gentrification' or wholesale demolition and rebuilding of 'failed' areas, but an approach that asks local people themselves to transform a place into a truly sustainable community. Another of Ecocity's most innovative aspects is its partnerships with over thirty organizations, which have enabled the activist project to mainstream its principles and contribute to sustainable development in the country on a much larger scale. The project found partners in the commercial sustainable development company Bioregional, the World Wildlife Fund, and, most importantly, in the City of Johannesburg, which has adopted the project as a municipal programme. To its great credit, this level of mainstreaming has been achieved without loss of the extraordinary level of innovation and participatory processes.

**Opposite** Cooperatives include a building company run by women, with intensive high-quality training provided by Ivory Park.

**Right** Other cooperatives include clothes-making and waste recycling as well as farming, bicycle repair and many other businesses. Almost all are run by women.

**Project Row Houses is an outstanding grassroots initiative that has used the cultural identity of a unique neighbourhood to regenerate the area without destroying or alienating the existing fragile community. Beginning primarily as an arts and cultural programme, it has expanded its remit to deal with the evolving pressures on one of the most historically important but deprived areas of Houston, Texas, and now encompasses housing, community development and education, as well as the participatory art programmes which began the project. Project Row Houses is a successful, multidimensional partnership between artists and a local community, working from the bottom-up to preserve and renew the unique cultural and social identity of the neighbourhood.**

**Above** The run-down row houses prior to the project's inception.

**Opposite** The Project Row Houses are located in one of the poorest areas of Houston, Texas.

Project Row Houses is located in the Third Ward area of Houston, Texas. Originally settled by freed slaves following the Civil War, the Third Ward was, until the 1960s, a thriving mixed-income neighbourhood, rich in African-American cultural heritage, including Houston's indigenous blues and jazz. 'Shotgun' (meaning row) houses are a Southern form of house design traditionally associated with such densely occupied neighbourhoods, their generous front porches encouraging an active street life and forming a distinctive urban grain. However, the end of housing segregation led to the eventual departure of upper- and middle-income African-American families. The resulting decline in income and education among residents remaining in the area led to Third Ward's designation by the City of Houston as a 'pocket of poverty'.

Project Row Houses (PRH) was established in 1993 by the artist Rick Lowe on a site of twenty-two abandoned shotgun houses to connect the work of artists with the revitalization of the community. It was inspired by the work of the African-American artist John Biggers who celebrated the social significance of the shotgun house community in his paintings. The programme now incorporates artist projects and residencies, housing and social services, education and community development, guided by a long-term masterplan for the renewal of the area. Of key importance to PRH has been the enticing of new families to the neighbourhood without gentrifying or forcing out the existing residents.

# Project Row Houses
## USA, 1993 – ongoing

The masterplan includes ten houses dedicated to art, photography and literary projects, which are programmed on a rotating six-month basis. When a group of artists is commissioned, each is given a house to transform in ways that speak of the history and cultural issues relevant to the African-American community. Adjacent to those dedicated to art, a Young Mothers Residential Program is located in seven houses and provides transitional housing and services for young mothers and their children, as a result of research into the housing needs of the community.

The further masterplanning of the area came about after PRH's first decade of successful arts and community programmes became threatened by the increasing gentrification of the inner-city areas. Since the early 1990s, inner-city Houston has experienced unprecedented development which has often resulted in the wholesale demolition of blocks of similar shotgun houses, decimating local cultural traditions and dislocating residents.

As the need for larger-scale neighbourhood planning became evident, PRH started to acquire more property in the neighbourhood, and set up the Row House District Collaborative, a group of artists and experts within and outside the Third Ward, to envision the community's future. They conducted neighbourhood surveys with the area's two schools, historic hospital, churches and local businesses, assessing both the physical state of the area and a needs assessment of local workers and families. They drew up principles and a neighbourhood plan as a tool for delivery, and created the Row Houses Community Development Corporation to implement the plan.

The Collaborative have drafted a plan which is seen as an evolving tool to enable the community to control its future development. This includes both physical improvements and capacity building among existing residents, aiming to retain the unique character of Third Ward while improving the homeownership rate. Additionally, to ensure a strong, viable community, the plan sets out to attract middle-income families to the Third Ward. The goal is the gradual development of a planned community including new and rehabilitated housing, pedestrian amenities, neighbourhood shops, and services that will unify the district's artistic and historic appeal. As part of this plan, four new duplexes were completed in October 2004, designed by the Rice Building Workshop, a group of students from Rice University in Houston who undertook the project as part of their training, thus also integrating the

**Above** Some of the new duplex buildings that now house single mothers, designed and built as part of the Rice Building Workshop, Rice University, Houston. They follow the forms of the earlier houses, so as to preserve the character of the area.

**Above** Some early installations in the row houses prior to their full renovation.

**Right** One of the paintings of the artist John Biggers, whose depictions of the row house communities inspired the genesis of the project.

development of the new housing with wider educational aims and processes. The Project Row Houses 'campus' now includes thirteen units of low-income housing, two of which are long-term artists' residences and two commercial buildings, which house the historic Eldorado Ballroom, an artist-initiated bike co-op and an artist residency/gallery space, alongside the original twenty-two shotgun houses.

Project Row Houses demonstrates a sensitive, bottom-up and incremental approach to community planning, which uses the cultural and historic identity of its location without resorting to a restrictively historicist programme. The artists' projects and residencies are key to this, as they provide a forward-looking and radical response to the area and actively engage the community with these concepts and provocations. Project Row Houses finds the fine balance between preservation and development by placing engagement and creativity at the heart of its processes.

**Opposite** Recent property speculation has led to Project Row Houses taking a more active role in community planning and regeneration.

**Below** The twenty-four houses now house art installations and residencies, social and education programmes, and a bike co-op, alongside provision of housing.

Elemental is a project to develop new low-cost housing designs, through an architectural competition and an initial demonstration project of 93 houses built by a specially formed architecture office. It is important for its organizational structure and strategy, but also for the approach to social housing that it has developed. Elemental approaches the provision of housing as a baseline service for individuals to adapt and extend as their social and economic conditions change – a response to the realization that development does not consist of a finite project, but rather is an ongoing process of transformation of which physical intervention is but one part.

**Opposite and below** The Elemental demonstration houses provide the infrastructure and essential services for a decent quality of life, but are designed to be expanded and modified by the resident over a longer time period, enabling personal expression and ownership, as well as a practical response to a tiny budget.

Elemental, based at the Universidad Católica de Chile and supported by a Chilean government grant and the Harvard Design School, is an initiative to construct seven exemplary projects of around two-hundred houses each, bringing together best practices in construction and engineering, social work and architecture. The project was founded by a group of architects and engineers in response to the current provision of social housing. Under a new government programme, grants had become available for the provision of housing for families with no financial resources, consisting of a $7,500 subsidy voucher per family intended to cover land, infrastructure and building cost. However, costs in the Chilean building industry meant that this budget could build only 25–30 square metres (270–320 square feet) of space so the beneficiaries of the programme had to resort to self-build to transform the grant they received into a full dwelling.

Elemental also grew out of a concern that much new social housing was being built in unsustainable ways. Looking for cheap land, lots tend to be at the periphery of the cities, far from the opportunities that might help families overcome poverty, creating belts of unemployment, resentment and violence. Current typologies generally use the most inexpensive house type – the isolated house in the middle of a lot, an inefficient use of land which increases sprawl and poverty belts. An alternative, more land-efficient, method is to build row houses with two floors. However, because the internal area that could be afforded is so small, this results in three- to four-metre- (10 to 13-foot) wide houses (the width of one room). Whenever a family wants to add a new room, it blocks access to light and ventilation in its other rooms,

# Elemental
Chile, 2001–ongoing

and efficiency gives way to overcrowding. The other current model is high-rise buildings, which block any possible expansion by the residents, condemning them to live in tiny spaces.

Elemental therefore redefined the problem of affordable housing provision in the following terms: sites should be better located within the network of opportunities in cities; a house type should be developed that, when multiplied to form a new housing area, contributes to a better quality of urban space; and the architecture should allow the easy and safe building of expansions. Elemental aimed to address the problem from several different angles: architectural design, engineering and construction (using development and lab tests for new prefabricated components and seismic systems), and social and community work (offering pre- and post-construction guidance to residents). The parts of the house that could be built for the original $7,500 should provide the elements that an individual homeowner's initiative would not be able to produce subsequently.

To get the best possible architecture, Elemental organized an international competition for professionals and students, which attracted more than 730 entries from all over the world. The prizewinners are being assisted by the Taller de Chile, a specifically assembled multidisciplinary group of practitioners (policy-making, engineering, architecture, urban design, planning) who provide logistical support and liaison with the communities benefiting from the design process and local building companies. Additionally, student winners of the competition were awarded financial support to travel from their country of origin to join the Taller.

The Taller also developed a demonstration housing project in the city of Iquique as a prototype demonstrating the principles of the Elemental approach to housing, providing housing for nearly one hundred families that for thirty years had illegally occupied a site near the city centre. The project keeps the community on the same plot of land, maintaining social and work ties. Technical and design support workshops were set up by Elemental's architects to help the inhabitants participate in the design and subsequently to extend and modify their spaces. The planning of the development favours the use of communal space by grouping the houses around courtyards of around twenty families. The ground floor units are built as flexible modules, which can expand horizontally, and those on the top floors can expand

vertically, so the building typology has just a ground and top floor. Sixty per cent of each unit's volume would eventually be self-built so the initial building provides a supporting structural framework for this construction.

Elemental has revitalized the issue of housing for the poor by proving the viability of a different approach to building under real conditions and constraints. It offers a different urban model to the current sprawl of South American city outskirts, of the favela. in the words of Alejandro Aravena, in an essay on the project in *Harvard Design Magazine*, it is 'not about making more beautiful houses, but about being intelligent in their configuration'. Elemental builds a scenario with the potential for change, where the architect is the mediator within social, technical and political processes.

The confidence that the government of Chile and the partner institutions have shown toward the initiative reaffirms the bridging role of the university in Chile's housing development. Perhaps the most significant element of this housing effort is that it supports its residents' future self-defined designs and building and thus also their sense of pride and ownership. This, together with the implications of its design – extended families living in collective spaces, urban centrality, and the creation of public spaces – makes housing not an end in itself but a tool for creating communities that have a long-term sustainability within the city.

**Above** The premise is that low-income families can gradually upgrade their homes as their situation improves, as opposed to the traditional scenario of expecting poor families to move on if they become wealthier, or being crammed into 'basic' homes that they cannot adapt. The houses provide decent accommodation with generous but basic internal spaces.

Play or Rewind demonstrates that in even the most precious and protected urban setting – the world heritage site of Siena – interventions for spontaneous, irreverent play can contribute to a fresh look at historic environments. Equally, areas that are seen as derelict or worthless can be used as pleasure gardens and play spaces, prompting a reappraisal of their value and highlighting their hidden beauty and importance. These playful interventions can be temporary or permanent and can involve much or little physical change to the space – the colonization of unpromising urban spaces by skateboarders, for example, has limited physical impact on the space but provides a performance spectacle in cities that brings new value to neglected and unused spaces.

**Right and opposite** Play or Rewind brought spontaneous and unexpected play into the historic city of Siena for one day.

Play or Rewind was an ephemeral installation in Siena by the architecture collaborative Cliostraat and graduate students from the Arsnova Academy. It was developed, installed, enjoyed and dismantled over the course of one weekend – a magical spectacle that disappeared as suddenly as it arrived.

The project sought to suggest the possibility of interaction between people and the historical fabric of the town in a playful and joyful manner – completely different from the sightseeing tourist mode. The city would not be a frozen museum, but an active ground for unplanned uses and amusements. The group laid out the markings for a volleyball pitch, soccer field and ten-pin bowling alley in three public squares in the city.

The project aimed to trigger unpredictable behaviour and spontaneous events, and unplanned interaction between strangers in the city – tourists and locals, young and old. Some rules (those of the three sports) were at the same time imposed and contradicted, as the boundaries of the sports fields took weird shapes in order to match with, intersect or overlap the urban spaces.

The three installations had an immediate impact. Hundreds of people – locals, passers-by, Italian and foreign tourists, children and adults – started spontaneously to enjoy those unusual and unexpected sports fields, playing volleyball, soccer and bowling. For a few hours, the historical core of Siena was turned into a playground.

Play is an overlooked part of contemporary city life and one of the most neglected aspects of the public realm. Opportunities for spontaneous

# Play or Rewind

Italy, 2001

action, surprise and pleasure for all age groups are being designed out of cities amid fears for safety, maintenance and cost, yet it is these aspects that make dense urban environments liveable and humane. Encouraging and prompting play makes public spaces safer and more cared for, by encouraging lingering and interaction with the space rather than merely using the public realm as a corridor. Design for pleasure and play enlivens public spaces and engages the age groups that are vital to the continued renewal of the city, encouraging interaction and creativity.

**Opposite** The games allowed an alternative vision of life in a 'museum' city.

**Below** Interaction with the civic space occurred for all ages, playing together.

**Above and opposite** The games brought
residents and tourists together, sparking the
imagination and suggesting that new life
could inhabit the historic city without damage
or disrespect.

# PROJECT INFORMATION

### UTILITY
Playpump, South Africa
Stanica, Slovakia
Landschaftspark Duisburg Nord, Germany
Xochimilco Park, Mexico
Slum Networking, India

### CITIZENSHIP
Edible Schoolyard, USA
CLEAN-India, India
Hotel Neustadt, Germany
Ala Plástica, Argentina
De Strip, The Netherlands

### RURAL
Nelson Mandela Museum, South Africa
Now Here: A Park for Las Aceñas, Spain
Rural Studio, USA
Cattle Tracks, Spain

### IDENTITY
Snow Culture Project, Japan
OASIS, USA
Invisible Zagreb, Croatia
Common Ground, UK

### URBAN
Mobile City Farm, USA
Ivory Park Ecocity, South Africa
Project Row Houses, USA
Elemental, Chile
Play or Rewind, Italy

# UTILITY

## Playpump 1997–ongoing

**Organization** Roundabout Outdoor is a fully commercial operation that installs Playpumps and maintains them on behalf of Roundabout Playpumps, the NGO branch of the operation which attracts funds from international foundations and donors in order to install Playpumps in previously disadvantaged communities. Financing is through the South African Department of Water as well as international foundations such as the Clinton Global Initiative, Henry J. Kaiser Family Foundation and ClearWater Project, and Coca-Cola.

**How it started** The concept was invented by Ronnie Styver, a drilling contractor, in the early 1990s. Roundabout Outdoor, an outdoor advertising company based in Johannesburg which entered into an agreement with Styver to obtain the exclusive rights to market the system locally and internationally, decided to throw its weight behind a campaign to help rural people receive clean water and began installing the pumps all over the country. The Playpump is now patented by Roundabout Outdoor Ltd and the pumps are manufactured locally at its factory in Springs, on the East Rand.

**Budget and funding** Each pump costs approx £4,500 (R50,000) to install and services up to 2,500 people. Roundabout Outdoor now have an annual budget of R7.5m to install pumps all over southern Africa.

**Results** Over 700 Playpumps installed since 1999, bringing water to over one million people across South Africa. Over the next few years, Roundabout hopes to reach ten million people.

**Awards**

World Bank's Development Marketplace Award in 2000; South Africa Mail and Guardian Investing in the Future Awards 2003

**Further information**

www.playpumps.org

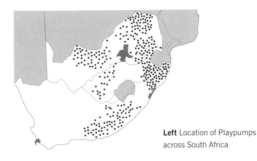

**Left** Location of Playpumps across South Africa

Architecture for Humanity (ed.), *Design like you give a damn*, New York, London, 2006
Steffen, A. (ed.), *Worldchanging: a User's Guide to the 21st Century*, New York, 2006

## Stanica 2001–ongoing

**Organization** Stanica is run by Truc Sphérique, a cultural non-profit organization working in arts and social engagement.

**How it started** Truc Sphérique initiated the project, with agreement from the railway company for a thirty-year lease on the building. They worked with young architects, landscape designers and interior designers who at the time had not yet left college and who worked for free, and with support from a professional architect and engineer who also waived their fees. Much of the building work was completed by over 200 volunteers.

**Budget and funding** Annual running budget €150,000 and construction budget of SKK10m. Funding for Truc Sphérique has been on a project basis from grants (including EU programmes, foundations including the Open Society Institute and Trust for Civil society, embassies and foreign cultural institutions). The Slovak Ministry of Culture now provides grant funding for the project but more than 50 per cent of the costs have been met by sponsorship,

voluntary work or donations. Now it is operational, the centre also provides some self-financing through its café, ticket sales, and Truc Sphérique's design studio and consulting services – altogether these income sources make up to 15–20 per cent of the annual budget.

**Timescale** The station began to be renovated in 2003 after two years of negotiation with the railway authorities, and the work is being completed in incremental stages. Performances and events have taken place from the beginning of the construction period in order to animate the space from the start – the first year of events was named Provisorium, and the second year named Work Demonstration, conveying the sense of the work in progress. By 2005 the centre was functionally complete although further stages of work will be completed on other parts of the building.

**Lead practitioners** Multidisciplinary artists and cultural practitioners, social workers, art therapists, architects and community workers.

**Results** Community cultural centre, artist studios, educational facilities and renovated train station.

**Further information**

www.stanica.sk
Adamov, M., 'Arts and urban change: the Zilina Project' *Policies for Culture Journal*, Winter 2003

## Landschaftspark Duisburg Nord 1989–ongoing

**How it started** The International Building Exhibition (IBA) Emscher Park in the Ruhr District was a major government-funded initiative to set quality building and planning standards for the environmental, economic and social transformation of an old industrialized region. It initiated around 120 projects in the region ranging from new housing to landscape and infrastructural works. The Duisburg Nord landscape park is one of these projects. Latz & Partners were selected from an international competition as the designers for the park.

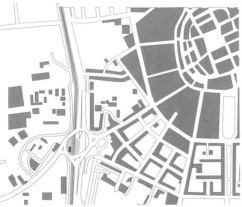

**Left** Location of Stanica, in the town of Zilina, Slovakia

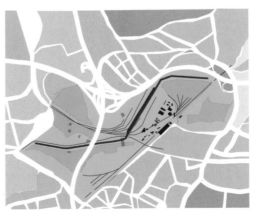

500m

**Left** Landschaftspark Duisburg Nord

**Client** Development Company North Rhine – Westphalia in trusteeship for the town of Duisburg, Emscher Cooperative Essen and Association of Communities Ruhr Essen.

**Budget** The park's budget was around €16m, not including decontamination operations or the construction of the subterranean sewer. 50 per cent of the park's maintenance costs are covered by letting of buildings and open spaces for special events, while the other 50 per cent are covered by the state (total annual maintenance costs including buildings is around €1.5m).

**Lead practitioners** Latz & Partners landscape architects.

**Results** The park employs 365 local people directly, with over 200 associated jobs, and receives over half a million outside visitors a year.

**Scale** 230 hectares (570 acres).

**Awards**

German Landscape Architecture Award, 2001.
EDRA/Places Award for Landscape, 2005

**Further information**

www.landschaftspark.de
Kirkwood, N. (ed.), *Manufactured Sites: Rethinking the Post-Industrial Landscape in the Urban Environment*, Oxford, 2001
Reed, P., *Groundswell: Constructing the Contemporary Landscape*, New York, 2005

Above Location of Xochimilco
Park on the outskirts of
Mexico City.

5km   10km

# Xochimilco Park 1989–93

**How it started** Declared a World Heritage Site by UNESCO in 1987, the cultural importance of the site helped prompt the clean-up efforts of the environmentally degraded site. Through the backing of environmental organizations, political support was garnered for the restoration of the waterfront and eventually President Salinas designated Xochimilco for 'ecological rescue.'

The project was a multi-million dollar investment completed between 1989–93 by various agencies of the Mexico City government and the borough of Xochimilco. The park is run by a non-profit 'Patronage of the Ecological Park of Xochimilco' and they rely on the private sector to support some of the educational activities.

**Funding** State funds

**Results** 3,000 hectares (7,414 acres) of ecological restoration and a 300-hectare (741-acre) ecological park within this, attracting over one million domestic and international visitors a year.

**Awards**

ASLA Award 1994
1996 Long Haul Special Award, BA World Tourism Awards
1996 Prince of Wales Green Prize in Urban Design, given by Harvard University Graduate School of Design

**Further information**

Truelove, J. G., *Ten Landscapes: Mario Schjetnan*, Glouster, Rockport, 2002
Beardsley, J., 'A Word for Landscape Architecture', in *Harvard Design Magazine*, Fall 2000

# Slum Networking 1987–ongoing

**How it started** British-trained engineer Himanshu Parikh was engaged by the UK Department for International Development (DFID) to work on a slum upgrading project that they were initiating with the Indore Development Authority to install basic sanitary provision to 450,000 slum dwellers. The Slum Networking process was first developed for Indore but has since been used in many cities around India and is currently being applied in 150 villages in Andra Pradesh province.

**Lead practitioner** Himanshu Parikh, structural engineer.

**Budget and funding** Slum Networking projects have been funded in many different ways, ranging from entirely grant funded (Indore was funded almost entirely by overseas development funding from DFID) to partnerships between the local government and a non-profit organization, or between government and industry, as in Ahmedabad. The slum dwellers themselves are always a capital partner in the project, paying between 2,000 and 4,000 rupees per household. The total cost per household is currently around 12,000 rupees.

Above Map of the slums (in black) in Indore, India, clustered next to the watercourses (blue).

■ Slums
■ Natural drainage courses
■ Pedestrian greens

**Timescale** The first Slum Networking project in Indore – covering 450,000 people – began in 1987 with the initial planning work. Site work started 1989 and was completed in 1997 with continual in-situ upgrading and extension of the works. Projects in other cities have taken a much shorter time period due to dealing with smaller slum pockets at a time: a recent project in Ahmedabad covering 1,000 people was completed in less than a year from the initiation of the project to full practical completion.

**Results** In total over one million slum dwellers have benefited from Slum Networking, gaining a normal level of street paving, water and sewage provision for the first time.

**Awards**

UN-Habitat World Award 1993
Aga Khan Award for Architecture, 1998
Best Practices by UNCHS, 1996 and 1998
Government of India Citation, 1998

**Further information:**

Himanshu Parikh, 'Slum Networking along the Indore River', *Architectural Design*, vol. 74 no. 2, 2004
CEPT, *Wealth and Well being Impacts of Slum Upgrading and Improved Service Delivery to the Poor, A Case study of Slum Networking Project*, Ahmedabad, India. Prepared by School of Planning, Submitted to Water and Sanitation Program-South Asia
World Bank, 2004
Tripathi, D., *Alliance for Change: A Slum Upgrading Experiment in Ahmedabad*, Tata McGraw-Hill, 1998
www.archnet.org

# CITIZENSHIP

## Edible Schoolyard 1994–ongoing

**Organization** Martin Luther King Jr Middle School, Berkeley, California.

**How it started** The project was initiated by chef Alice Waters, founder of the world-famous restaurant Chez Panisse, and the then-head of the school, Neil Smith, in collaboration with teachers and members of the community. The school hosted a symposium, inviting landscape architects, chefs, gardeners, teachers, and other design professionals to share their visions of a future garden. The school owned an abandoned lot adjacent to the school that was selected as the site. No 'garden designers' were involved but architectural students volunteered to build the shade structures in the garden, and professional designers worked on the conversion of an 1940s bungalow into the new kitchen classroom. The Edible Schoolyard is a non-profit organization separate from the school.

**Budget and funding** The Edible Schoolyard has been funded entirely through private foundations and family foundations. In the first year its budget was $10,000, and this sum has risen to $300,000 currently for the city-wide programme (the ES employs 8 full-time staff). The building of the kitchen classroom was funded partly by a waste reduction grant from Alameda County Waste Management and reused fixtures from the old building to reduce cost and teach about sustainability. The School Lunch Initiative is being funded jointly by the Chez Panisse Foundation, the Center for Ecoliteracy and the Berkeley Unified School District board.

**Timescale** The process of planning the Edible Schoolyard began in 1994, with the symposium held in 1995. Work on clearing the site began in late 1995 and the first cover crop was planted in 1996. The school has continued to run and expand its programmes in relation to the garden and kitchen ever since.

**Results** A one-acre working garden and kitchen classroom, which every student in the 900-strong school participates in every year. The site now includes a shade shelter, fully equipped kitchen building, outdoor oven, chicken coop and composting.

**Awards**
Alice Waters received an 'Excellence in Education' award from the state of California and a U.S. Department of Education 'Educational Heroes' award.
The kitchen classroom won International Design Magazine's 2002 Design Distinction Contest, in the Environmental Category.

**Further information**
www.edibleschoolyard.org
Stone, M. K., 'A Food Revolution in Berkeley,' *Whole Earth Magazine*, Spring 2003
Schlosser, E., and C. Wilson, *Chew On This: Everything You Don't Want to Know About Fast Food*, Boston, 2006

## CLEAN-India 1996–ongoing

**How it started** The programme began in 1996 as CLEAN-Delhi, a project by Development Alternatives, an Indian NGO, which had been running programmes in the field of environmental education for several years. Development Alternatives has continued to be the umbrella organization for the programme and CLEAN-India uses its workshops, labs and research capacity. The success of the project led to partners initiating the programme in cities across the country, rapidly scaling up to the current level of action.

**Budget and funding** Initial seed funding from Development Alternatives. The European Commission committed a five-year block of funding to the programme in 2001 consisting of €905,000 per year, to enable it to roll out programmes in more cities across the country.

**Lead practitioners** Ecologists and environmental campaigners.

**Scale** 35 cities and 286 schools across India.

**Further information**
www.cleanindia.org
Global Knowledge Partnership, *Youth, Poverty, Gender: ICT for development success stories*, Kuala Lumpur, 2003

## Hotel Neustadt 2002–2003

**How it started** Initiated by Thalia, the state-funded young people's theatre in Halle, and Raumlabor, an architectural and urbanism office from Berlin. The project grew out of a previous project that the two organizations had produced which involved 7–14-year-old children, and research that Raumlabor had been doing for the city on how to deal with the complex area of Halle-Neustadt in the future.

**Left** Location of Edible Schoolyard within the Martin Luther King Middle School, Berkeley, California

**Left** The CLEAN-India network of cities.

**Budget and funding** The budget for the whole project was €250,000. The project's principal funder was the German Cultural Foundation. In-kind support came from many large and small sponsors, providing everything from building materials to cups donated by individuals for use in the hotel café. Each room was renovated for only €2.35 – the rest of the materials were donated or reclaimed at no cost.

**Timescale** The preparation for the project took around a year, including preparatory events to attract teenagers to the site, and raise the local level of interest in the project. The Hotel was open from 25 August to 3 October 2003. The festival ran from 18 September to 3 October 2003.

**Lead practitioners** Thalia Theater Halle, Raumlabor architects, 137 artists, over 120 teenagers.

**Results** A temporary hotel with 92 rooms and 80 per cent average occupancy, and an arts festival. There were over 8,700 visitors to the project.

**Further information**
www.hotel-neustadt.de
Thalia Theater Halle (ed.), *Hotel Neustadt*, Berlin, 2004
Ferguson, F. (ed.), *Deutschlandscape: German Pavilion, 9th International Architecture Exhibition 2004 – Venice Biennale* (exh. cat.), Ostfildern, 2004

## Ala Plástica 1995–ongoing

**Organization** Ala Plástica is an ecology collaborative.

**How it started** Ala Plástica initiated the Bioregional Initiative in 1995 after an earlier project on natural reedbeds and waste filtration. Ala Plástica collaborates with a huge number of other organisations from informal community groups, local farmers and artisans, to international NGOs and the local regional authorities. It uses art projects as a way to focus on local communities' creativity and to build networks that might not otherwise be possible. The projects of the Bioregional Initiative have involved organized groups of the local, cooperative community, municipalities, art agencies and in some cases the financing comes from these sources.

**Budget and funding** Support for the initial projects in the Rio de la Plata basin came from the British Council and subsequent projects have been funded by grants from a variety of organizations. Project AA (Ala Plástica's latest programme) has an operational budget for equipment, materials, services, mobility and fees of £19,200.

**Timescale** The Bioregional initiative started in 1995. Project AA has a timescale of 63 weeks.

**Lead practitioners** Ala Plástica comprises Alejandro Meitin (artist and lawyer) Silvina Babich (artist and teacher) and Rafael Santos (artist). Collaborators include biologists, botanists, designers, a web programmer, a social anthropologist, PR planner and a 'rural producer'. Other people and institutions are involved at different times in the project.

**Further information**
www.alaplastica.org.ar
Benjamín, W., *Imaginación y Sociedad*, Taurus, 1999
Dillemuth, S., *The Academy and the Corporate Public*, Bergen/London 2002
Gerz, J., *Res Publica, L´Opera Pubblica 1968–1999*, Museion Bolzano, 1999

## De Strip 2002–2004

**How it started** Artist Jeanne van Heeswijk was commissioned by the clients to brighten up the facade of a row of vacant shops that were due to be demolished. She had already been working on the project Until We Meet again and knew the area well, and therefore devised a programme that went beyond the brief and used the insides of the shops as spaces for cultural production.

Van Heeswijk asked the Museum Boijmans Van Beuningen and MAMA, Showroom for Media and Moving Art, to contribute, a young architect and construction firm worked together to renovate the shops. Van Heeswijk also worked with the housing association and the Welfare Office to reach as many residents as possible and include them fully in the project.

**Client** The Waterweg Housing Corporation and the City of Vlaardingen.

**Budget and funding** The total budget for the programme was €588,600. Funding came from the client and the Facilitaire Dienst City of Vlaardingen, the Educational dept. City of Vlaardingen, Province of South Holland.

**Lead practitioner** Artist. There were 319 collaborators in total including; community, artists, seven galleries (part of the program for De Strip consisted of the opening of a branch of Boijmans Van Beuningen Museum in three of the former shops), craftsmen (studios were created where craftsmen worked for a period of three months where instead of paying rent they gave workshops twice a week).

**Results** De Strip occupied a 3,500m2 building divided into 7 spaces. The two year project culminated in 102 projects visited by 46,000 people.

**Further information**
www.destrip-westwijk.net
Van Heeswijk, J., *Jeanne van Heeswijk: De Strip 2002–2004 Westwijk, Vlaardingen*, Amsterdam, 2004
Pietromarchi, B. (ed), *The [un]common place – art, public space and urban aesthetics in Europe*, Barcelona, 2005.
Purves, T. (ed.), *What We Want is Free: Experiments with Exchange and Generosity in Current Art*, New York, 2004
www.videomagazijn.org
www.worldwidewestwijk.nl

100m 200m

**Left** The Westwijk area of Vlaardingen, location of De Strip (red).

# RURAL

## Nelson Mandela Museum 1997–2006

**How it started** The museum was started soon after Nelson Mandela was elected president. He made it known that he would keep the gifts that he was given in trust for the nation, and eventually house them in a facility near his birthplace in rural South Africa. Mandela had a strong vision for a museum that would have social benefits for his birthplace and home region.

**Client** National Department of Sports, Arts and Culture, South Africa.

**Funding** Both capital and revenue costs are funded by central government.

**Date and timescale** The first parts of the museum opened in 2000, and the final part – the Qunu Youth Centre – opened in 2006.

**Lead practitioners** Nina Cohen and Hilton Judin, architects and curators.

**Results** A new museum on three sites, with training, community and social facilities, increasing local tourism and alleviating poverty.

**Further information**
www.mandelamuseum.org.za
Judin, H., 'Cohen & Judin: Nelson Mandela Museum in Umtata/ Qunu/Mvezo, South Africa' in *Architektur Aktuell*, issue 245, 2000

## Now Here: A Park for Las Aceñas 1999

**How it started** c a l c were invited in 1999 by the O.K Center for Contemporary Art in Linz, Austria to participate in an exhibition with the title: 'Things Between Life, Art and Work' and Now Here, with the 'orange art', was their contribution to the exhibition.

**Funding** The purchase of 500 square metres (5,800 square feet) of land was €8,000, covered by the fee from producing the exhibition in Linz which itself was grant funded. Ongoing maintenance costs are covered by Navia's council, and the yearly village party (which includes; children's theatre, projections, bar and bands) is financed by the takings from the bar, run by c a l c.

**Lead practitioners** Artist, multimedia and architectural collective.

**Results** New public park. Since the transformation of the village centre, c a l c and the people of Las Aceñas are continuing to expand and improve the village's social infrastructures. This includes current plans to convert an ex-slaughter house into a social club, with a bar, games, cinema and children's playground.

**Awards**
Special prize of the jury for Minimum Prize, Cittadellarte, Fondazione Pistoletto

**Further information**
Bianchi, P., *LKM – Things Between Life, Art and Work*, Linz, 1999
www.calcaxy.com

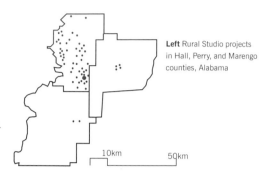

**Left** Rural Studio projects in Hall, Perry, and Marengo counties, Alabama

10km    50km

## Rural Studio 1993–ongoing

**Organization** The Rural Studio is an elective studio as part of Auburn University's B.Arch programme and also a registered non-profit organization. The studio is an elective choice for 2nd and 5th year architecture students who apply and are selected to spend one semester (2nd year) or their thesis year (5th year) in Hale County. It also operates a one-year non-credit programme for students from mixed disciplines who wish to participate.

**How it started** Rural Studio was set up by Samuel Mockbee and D. K. Ruth, practising architects and teachers at Auburn University.

**Clients** The first clients for houses were selected by the Department of Human Resources of Hale County but as this was not always successful, now the clients for the houses are selected by a committee of faculty and staff of the Rural Studio and Hale County community leaders. Community projects have generally been brought by community groups to the Rural Studio although in some cases the studio has approached organizations with proposals, where it has seen a need or an opportunity. The students work closely with the clients on the brief for the community buildings, which has often resulted in changes as the students have raised the aspirations of the client and their awareness of what might be possible.

Individual client bodies have included the Hale Empowerment and Revitalization Organization (HERO), the Perry Lakes Park, the Perry County School Board, the Thomaston Rural Heritage Center, Newbern Tigers baseball team,

**Budget and funding** Initially the Rural Studio received no financial support from Auburn University and was entirely funded by donations of money or materials, resulting in an aesthetic that prioritized innovative and cost-saving construction, recycled or free materials, and relatively small projects. All the buildings that are used by the Rural Studio were donated to it.

Currently, the Rural Studio's eight staff and overheads are covered by Auburn (a cost of $400,000 p.a.). The projects themselves are funded entirely by private donations and grants. The Studio receives around $200,000 a year in this way, which all the projects (usually five major projects a year plus 'neck-down' home repair or renovation projects) share. In addition the students raise support through donations of materials, fundraising, grants and

in-kind support. The clients for the community projects often fund most of the cost of the project but in some cases major fundraising has been achieved by the students: the recently completed firestation raised nearly $100,000 in donations and in-kind support.

**Results** Over fifty community projects and fifteen houses completed in three counties in West Alabama.

**Awards**
Samuel Mockbee received a MacArthur 'Genius Grant' for the Rural Studio's work and the American Institute of Architects Gold Medal. Various individual buildings have also won awards.

**Further information**
www.ruralstudio.org
Oppenheimer Dean, A., and T. Hursley, *Proceed and be bold: Rural Studio After Samuel Mockbee*, New York, 2005
Oppenheimer Dean, A., and T. Hursley, *Rural Studio: Samuel Mockbee and an Architecture of Decency*, New York, 2002
Mockbee, S., and the Rural Studio, *Community Architecture*, Birmingham, 2002

## Cattle Tracks 1998–2002

**Client** Municipality of Osuna

**How it started** The project was initiated due to the extensive network of ancient tracks in the Osuna area having been largely lost and destroyed. The project was started by the municipal government of the Osuna area and developed in partnership with regional and national public funding. Other organizations, such as the local scouts groups, ecological groups, the university and farmers became involved in the mapping and restoration project.

**Budget and funding** The total cost was €1.1m which was jointly funded by the local council, the rural development group (Sierra Sur), the local authority, and regional and central government.

**Date and timescale** The project began with the ratification (1996–2000) of the cooperation agreement for administration, ordering and recovery of the Osuna cattle tracks. This was extended in 2001. The physical works began in 1999 and were largely complete by 2002 although they continue to be extended.

**Lead practitioners** Ecologists, local archaeologists and historians.

**Results** The restoration and signposting of 400km (250 miles) of ancient cattle tracks. Water troughs, benches and tree planting to aid ecological restoration and public access. Employment and training for local low-income groups, and an increase in eco-tourism locally.

**Scale** 400km (250 miles) of cattle tracks.

**Awards**
2002 United Nations award for Best Practice

# IDENTITY

## Snow Culture Project 1986–ongoing

**Organization** The municipal government of Yasuzuka. The Snowman Foundation is a non-profit organization that runs the research and education programmes, and coordinates the snow-related development.

**How it started** The long-term series of projects was initiated in the first instance by the municipality. A town ordinance was passed designating the 'snow culture village', and the Snowman Foundation was set up as the coordinating agency. It was responsible for researching and initiating projects including its own new building by Jun Aoki – suggesting briefs and working with the town council.

**Range of practitioners involved** Planners, ecologists and environmentalists, scientists, engineers, agriculturalists, architects, community leaders.

**Results** Over 100,000 tourists now visit Yasuzuka each year, brought by the unique snow culture, recreational facilities and attractions. The population has stabilized its decline. New elementary school, community and cultural centre, research facility, warehouses for food storage, ballpark, skifields, hot springs, tourist facilities, etc have been built.

**Awards**
Japan Planning Award, Prime Minister's Award (1995)

**Further information**
www.yukidaruma.or.jp
Aoki, J., *Atmospherics*, Tokyo, 2000
Partap, Dr Tej (ed.), *Evolving Sustainable Production Systems in Sloping Upland Areas – Land Classification Issues and Options*, APO, 2004

## OASIS 2000–ongoing

**Organization** OASIS is a coalition of non-profit organizations, agencies, businesses, grassroots groups, educational institutions, and New York City residents. The partnership includes federal agencies, state/local agencies such as the New York State Department of Environmental Conservation and NYC Department of Parks & Recreation, and non-governmental participants including businesses, non-profit organizations and institutions such as Columbia University.

**How it started** The project was initiated by the USDA Forestry Service. Other founding partners in the project were the USDA Natural Resources Conservation Service, the NYC Dept of Parks and Recreation, Environmental Systems Research Institute, Inc., and the New York Restoration Project. The technical work and day-to-day management of the maps has been undertaken by the NY Public Interest Research Group's Community Mapping Assistance Project, a non-profit organization.

**Funding** Funded initially by the USDA Forest Service and Natural Resources Conservation Service. Environmental Systems Research Institute, Inc. (ESRI) donated staff time and software, and many other city and state agencies also gave in-kind support. OASIS is managed by NYPIRG, a non-profit organization.

**Results** OASIS covers all of New York City. The website is accessed more than 25,000 times per week and is used to make more than a million maps a year.

**Awards**
The Forest Service's 2004 Chief's Award for Technology Transfer, 2004
Municipal Art Society's Certificate of Merit, 2001

**Further information**
www.oasisnyc.org
Maantay, J., and J. Ziegler, *GIS for the Urban Environment*, New York, 2006

## Invisible Zagreb 2003–2005

**How it started** The project was started as an independent project by Platforma 9,81, a young architecture group dedicated to public engagement with planning and urban change in Zagreb. Platforma 9,81 collaborated closely with the city and other artist and architecture groups as the project became part of the wider programme 'Zagreb: Cultural Kapital of Europe 3000'.

**Funding** City of Zagreb, Ministry of Culture of the Republic of Croatia, German Federal Cultural Foundation, 'Kontakt', the Arts and Civil Society Program of Erste Bank Group in Central Europe.

**Timescale** The project was a two-year programme of events and installations.

**Lead practitioners** Platforma 9,81, an architect-artist collaborative.

**Further information**
Mrduljas, M., 'Invisible Zagreb', *Oris: Magazine for Architecture and Culture*, vol. 8, no. 38, 2006
www.platforma981.hr

## Common Ground 1982–ongoing

**Organization** Common Ground is a small non-profit organization based in rural Dorset, England.

**How it started** Common Ground was founded by Sue Clifford and Angela King in 1982 as an independent campaigning charity.

**Funding** Funded by public and private grants and donations. Specific projects sometimes funded by central or local government, particularly the Department for the Environment.

**Results** Campaigns, books, initiatives, artist commissions, toolkits and advisory services. Common Ground invented Apple Day in 1990 and by 1999 over 600 events nationally celebrated it. It continues to grow.

**Further information**
www.commonground.org.uk
Clifford, S., and A. King, *England in Particular*, London, 2006
Clifford, S., and A. King, *Local Distinctiveness: place, particularity and identity*, Common Ground, 1993
The Common Ground Book of Orchards, Common Ground, 2000

# URBAN

## Mobile City Farm 1999–ongoing

**Organization** Resource Center Chicago is a registered non-profit organization.

**How it works** Mobile City Farm is a self-initiated project by the Resource Center. The city administration has allowed the Resource Centre to use city-owned land for free before it is redeveloped, as well as access to the water hydrants for irrigation. The design for the Mobile Farmstead arose from a workshop that the architects attended alongside the director of the Resource Center and was then further developed for the Chicago Sustainable Design Challenge.

**Budget and funding** A 0.4 hectare (one-acre) site requires a set-up cost of $20,000 covering compost, fencing and ground preparation, and a yearly running cost of $20,000. It can bring in $30,000 in sales of produce per year. The budget for the Mobile Farmstead is $15,000.

The project is funded through the Resource Center, private donations, donations in-kind and support from companies and the city such as free horse manure from the mounted police. It is run by mostly volunteer labour, reducing costs.

**Timescale** The first city farm was started in 1999. A new site can be up and running within one month of acquiring the right to use the land. The Mobile City Farmstead is due to be completed in early 2006.

**Lead practitioners** Community activists.

**Results** The project has set up city farms on around six sites so far. It currently operates four sites ranging from 1/4 acre to 1 acre.

**Awards**
1st Place Vegetable Garden, Mayor Daley's 2003 Landscape Awards
2003 Chicago Tribune Good Eating Award
2004 Chicago Sustainable Design Challenge - Award for Design Excellence

**Further information**
www.resourcecenterchicago.org
Bloom and A. Bromberg (eds), *Belltown Paradise/Making Their Own Plans*, Chicago, 2004
Evans, T., and C. Wheelan, *Revealing Chicago*, New York, 2005
Ableman, M., *Fields of Plenty*, San Francisco, 2005

## Ivory Park Ecocity 1993–ongoing

**How it started** A group of environmentalists and social activists initiated the project after a major chemical fire in the area in 1992 mobilized local people. The Ecocity Trust was founded in 2000. In 2002 the local council was amalgamated into the Johannesburg City Council who now 'own' the Ivory Park project. Bioregional and the World Wildlife Fund became partners in the project in 2002 and brought on board Arup as designers and engineers for the initial demonstration eco-village. Ecocity also works with a local architect, Ken Stucke, and many other local practitioners across disciplines. The Ecocity Trust now has offices in the council buildings and works on mainstreaming the principles behind the Ivory Park Ecocity into other projects across the country, in partnership with over 30 organizations and government agencies.

**Budget and funding** Initial funding (11m rand) came from the Danish government. The Ivory Park Ecocity has seen an investment of 30m rand over its eight years, which includes all infrastructure, decontamination, construction costs, training and capacity building and administration. Although significant initial funding came from overseas sources, most funding now comes from South African sources, including local and national government, and independent grants. Donor funding was raised from Danced (Danish Agency for Environment and Development), the Global Environmental Forum and other international funding agencies. Partnerships were also forged with local companies such as Eskom (the major power utility company) on specific projects such aspects of the house-building. Many of these funding agencies, grant agencies and indeed the national, provincial and local governments of South Africa have played a major role, both in terms of human resources and through financing.

**Timescale** The Ecocity concept originated in 1993.

**Lead practitioners** Local activists and environmentalists.

**Results** Over 300 jobs have been directly created, and over 4,000 people indirectly benefit from the Ecocity. The new youth training/housing programme now trains 450 youth each year. 3,000 bicycles have been sold, enabling their owners to access employment. 1,500 children have been trained in permaculture. Over 70 farmers, mostly women, are growing organic food for the community. Six agricultural cooperatives have been formed. 40 people have been employed in waste collection and waste sorting. 10 people are employed in making paper from waste paper and alien vegetation. An eco-village consisting of 30 houses, workshops and a community centre is built. Fourteen women have been trained in eco-building technologies such as grey waste-water treatment and water harvesting.

**Scale** Ivory Park has a population of 250,000.

**Awards**
UN-HABITAT award, 2000
SB'04 Sustainable Building Commendation 2004
Urban Renewal Award 2001

**Further information:**
www.ecocity.org.za

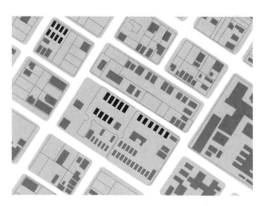

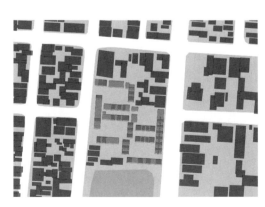

**Left** Project Row Houses: the original twenty-two houses (red) and new duplexes (orange)

**Left** Plan of Elemental housing, Quinta de Monroy, Chile

## Project Row Houses 1993–ongoing

**How it started** Initiated by Rick Lowe, a visual artist working in the area, and six other African-American artists in conjunction with Diverse Works, an alternative art space in the area. They acquired the twenty-two shotgun houses with the aid of a local family foundation, and renovated them initially entirely with volunteers – themselves, other artists and neighbourhood organizations. The Young Mothers residential programme grew from research by one of the members of the group into housing needs in the area, and was set up by Project Row Houses itself.

As the need for larger-scale neighbourhood planning became evident, PRH set up the Row House District Collaborative, a group of artists and experts within and outside the Third Ward. The Row Houses Community Development Corporation was then set up to implement the plan that the RHDC developed, and throughout there has been strong collaboration with Rice University architecture and planning departments.

**Budget and funding** Initial funding came from individual donations and grants, including the National Endowment for the Arts. The renovation of the initial 22 houses cost around $380,000 and was primarily funded by corporate sponsors as well as non-profit organizations and donors. Ongoing funding comes from a range of public and private sources and amounts to around $350,000 a year.

**Timescale** PRH started in 1993, taking a year to open the first eight houses. The Row Houses CDC was set up in 2003, and the first duplexes were completed in October 2004.

**Lead practitioners** Artists and community activists.

**Results** Twenty-two renovated shotgun houses containing artists' residencies and a Young Mothers residential and welfare programme, 13 units of low-income housing, two of which are long-term artists' residences and two commercial buildings, one of which houses the historic Eldorado Ballroom, an artist-initiated bike co-op, and an artist residency/gallery space.

**Scale** Project Row Houses works in 74 acres comprising 35 city blocks, which house around 400 households and 15 businesses as well as other activities, including seven churches.

**Awards**
NCARB Prize for 'creative integration of practice and education' in 2004.
Heinz Family Foundation prize, 2002
American Architectural Association Keystone Award, 2000.

**Further information:**
www.projectrowhouses.org
'A foundation for home building: Project Row Houses' in *Builder Magazine*, January 1, 1996
Ingersoll, R., *Sprawltown: Looking for the City on its Edges*, 2006
Gastil, R., *Open: New Designs for Public Space*, 2004
Anthony, K. H., *Designing for Diversity: Gender, Race, and Ethnicity in the Architectural Profession*, 2001

## Elemental 2001–ongoing

**Organization** Elemental and its associated architecture practice, the Taller de Chile, is a non-profit organization based at the School of Architecture, la Pontificia Universidad Católica de Chile, Santiago.

**How it started** In March 2001, the founders of Elemental met the Chilean Minister of Housing to suggest ideas and projects to alleviate the social housing problem. It was suggested that the group tackle the new housing policy under which low-income families were eligible for a $7,500 housing grant. As a result, a group of professors from the Harvard Design School, the Universidad Católica de Chile, the Housing Ministry of Chile, and Harvard's David Rockefeller Center of Latin American Studies, along with Chilean construction companies and social institutions, began to develop the project.

**Lead practitioners** Architects and engineers.

**Funding** The administration of the initiative is funded by the Chilean government, with sponsorship from some construction companies. The demonstration project was supported by the Chile-Barrio programme of the regional government but paid for under the new VSDsD grant programme. The project budget is $7,500 per house.

**Timescale** The competition was held in 2003 and the winners were announced in 2004. The Quinta de Monroy demonstration project was begun in 2002 and constructed from 2004–2005.

**Results** Seven housing projects of around 200 houses each.

**Further information**
www.elementalchile.org
Gallanti, F., 'Elemental, Aravena!' in *Domus*, 886, November 2005
Architecture for Humanity (ed.), *Design like you give a damn*, London, New York, 2006

## Play or Rewind 2001

**How it started** Cliostraat was asked by the director of the Arsnova Academy to develop an urban installation project, to be realized in the city of Siena with their graduate students. The Milan-based designer Tim Power was also involved. The initial concepts were discussed, refined and realized in Siena during a two-day weekend workshop in June 2001.

**Client** Arsnova Accademia di Arti Multimediali (Academy of Multimedia Arts), Siena, Italy

**Budget** Approximately €250. The sports equipment – volleyball nets and mini-soccer goalposts – were borrowed from a local athletic team.

**Timescale** On the first day, the students discussed and designed the project, chose sites and assembled the required materials. On the morning of the second day, the games were laid out and for the rest of the day, enjoyed by the public. Late at night on the second day, the equipment was removed and the sites left as before.

**Lead practitioners** Cliostraat is an art and architecture collaborative.

**Further information**
www.cliostraat.com
AAVV. 'Intro - Le Porte di Siena'. (Arsnova, Accademia delle Arti Multimediali, Siena, 2002)

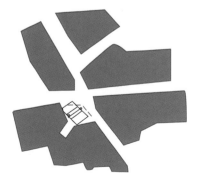

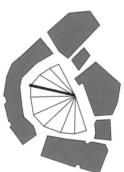

**Left** Plans of the locations of the Play or Rewind installation, Siena

# FURTHER READING AND RESOURCES

Peter Ackroyd, *London: The Biography*, London, 2000

Aga Khan Award for Architecture, www.akdn.org

Lady Allen of Hurtwood, *Planning for Play,* London, 1968

Architecture for Humanity (ed.), *Design like you give a damn: Architectural Responses to Humanitarian Crisis*, New York and London, 2006

ArchNet, www.archnet.org

Hannah Arendt, *The Human Condition*, Chicago & London, 1958

Bryan Bell (ed.), *Good deeds, Good design: Community service through architecture*, New York, 2004

Marshall Berman, *All That Is Solid Melts Into Air: Experience of Modernity*, London, 2000

Filip de Boeck and Marie-Françoise Plissart, *Kinshasa: Tales of the Invisible City (Exhibition Catalogue)*, Ghent-Amsterdam, 2004

Nicholas Bourriaud, *Relational Aesthetics,* France, 1998 (English translation 2002)

Dr Claudia Büttner and the City of Munich, Culture Department(ed.), *Kunstprojecte_riem: Public Art for a Munich District (Catalogue)*, Vienna, 2004

Building and Social Housing Foundation, www.bshf.org

Cabinet Magazine www.cabinetmagazine.org

Centre For Land Use Interpretation, www.clui.org

*Cities. Architecture and Society, 10th International Architecture Exhibition 2006-Venice Biennale (Exhibition Catalogue)*, Venice, 2006

Common Ground, *The Common Ground Book of Orchards: Conservation, Culture and Community*, London, 2000

Common Ground: Sue Clifford, Angela King, *England In Particular: A Celebration of the Commonplace, the Local, the Vernacular and the Distinctive,* London, 2006

Mike Davis, *City of Quartz: Excavating the Future in Los Angeles*, London, 1990

——, *Planet of Slums*, New York-London, 2006

Jared Diamond, *Collapse: New Societies Choose to Fail or Succeed*, New York, 2003

Roger Fawcett-Tang (ed.), *Mapping: An illustrated Guide to Navigational Systems*, Mies, Switzerland, 2002

Kenneth Frampton, 'Towards a Critical Regionalism: Six Points for an Architecture of Resistance', in Hal Foster (ed.), *Postmodern Culture*, London and Sydney, 1983

Francesca Ferguson (ed.), *Deutschlandscape: German Pavilion, 9th International Architecture Exhibition 2004-Venice Biennale (Exhibition Catalogue)*, Ostfildern, Germany, 2004

Richard Florida, *The Rise of the Creative Class: And How It's Transforming Work, Leisure, Community and Everyday Life*, New York, 2002

Deborah Gans and Claire Weisz (eds), *Extreme Sites: the 'Greening' of Brownfield*, Architectural Design, Vol 74, No 2, Chichester, March/April 2004

Jan Gehl, *Life Between Buildings: Using Public Space*, Copenhagen, 1996

Jan Gehl and Lars Gemzøe, *Public Spaces – Public Life*, Copenhagen, 1996

——, *New City Spaces*, Copenhagen, 2000

Herbert Girardet, *The Gaia Atlas of Cities: New Directions for Sustainable Urban Living*, London, 1992

——, *Schumacher Briefing No2: Creating Sustainable Cities*, Dartington, 1999

——, *Cities, People, Planet*, Chichester, 2004

David Gissen (ed.), *Big & Green: Toward Sustainable Architecture in the 21st Century*, New York, 2002

*Global Urban Indicators Database*, The United Nations Centre for Human Settlements (UN HABITAT), 2002

Al Gore, *An Inconvenient Truth: The Planetary Emergency of Global Warming and What We Can Do About It*, London, 2006

Dennis Hardy, *Utopian England: Community Experiments 1900-1945,* London, 2000

Jeanne van Heeswijk (ed.), *Westwijk, Vlaardingen 2002-2004: De Strip*, Amsterdam, 2004

Mark Hewitt and Susannah Hagan, *City Fights: Debates on Urban Sustainability*, London, 2001

Carl Honoré, *In Praise of Slow: How a Worldwide Movement Is Challenging the Cult of Speed*, London, 2004

Johan Huizinga, *Homo Ludens: A Study of the Play Element in Culture*, Boston, 1955

*International Building Exhibition Rotterdam-Hoogvliet: Wimby!- Welcome into My Backyard! (Exhibition Catalogue)*, Rotterdam, 2000

Mary Jane Jacob with Michael Brenson, *Conversations at the Castle: Changing audiences and contemporary art,* Cambridge (Mass.), 1998

Jane Jacobs, *The Death and Life of Great American Cities*, New York, 1993

Jeffrey Kastner and Brian Wallis, *Land and Environmental Art*, London, 1998

Sunjung Kim, Heejin Kim, Jang Un Kim (ed.), *Secret Beyond the Door: The Korean Pavilion, The 51st Venice Biennale (Exhibition Catalogue)*, Korea: The Korean Culture and Arts Foundation, 2005

Miwon Kwon, *One Place after Another: Site-Specific Art and Locational Identity,* Cambridge (Mass.), 2004

E. Layton and J. Blanco White, *The School Looks Around,* 1948

Liane Lefaivre and Ingeborg de Roode (ed.), *Aldo van Eyck: The Playgrounds and the City (Exhibition Catalogue)*, Rotterdam, 2002

Hans Loidl and Stefan Bernard, *Opening spaces: Design as Landscape Architecture*, Basel, 2003

Geert Mak, *Jorwerd: the death of the village in late C20th Europe*, London, 2000.

Mark Magazine www.mark-magazine.com

David Marquand, *Decline of the Public,* Cambridge, 2004

Bruce Mau and the Institute without Boundaries, *Massive Change*, London, 2004

Anna Minton, *What kind of world are we building? The privatisation of public space,* London, The Royal Institution of Chartered Surveyors, 2006

www.myvillages.org

Nils Norman, *An Architecture of Play: A Survey of London's Adventure Playgrounds*, London, 2003

Andrea Oppenheimer Dean and Timothy Hursley, *Rural Studio: Samuel Mockbee and an Architecture of Decency*, New York, 2002

——, *Proceed and be bold: Rural Studio After Samuel Mockbee*, New York, 2005

Philipp Oswalt, *Shrinking Cities: Vol.1 – International Research*, Germany, 2005

Sergio Palleroni and Christina Eichbaum Merkelbach, *Studio at large: Architecture in Service of Global Communities*, Seattle, 2004

PEER, *Art for All? Their Policies and our Culture*, editors: Mark Wallinger and Mary Warnock, London, 2000.

Public Works, *If You Can't Find It, Give Us a Ring*, Birmingham, 2006

Robert Puttnam, *Bowling Alone: The Collapse and Revival of American Community*, New York, 2001

Stephen Read, Jürgen Rosemann and Job van Eldijk (ed.), *Future City*, London, 2005

Richard Rogers, *Cities for a Small Planet*, London, 1997

—— and Prof. Anne Power, *Cities for a Small Country*, 2000

Ralph Rugoff (ed.), *Monuments for the USA,* San Francisco, 2005

Simon Sadler *The Situationist City*, Cambrdige (Mass.), 1998

Helena Sandman (ed.), *Jigeen Yi Mbooloo*, Helsinki, Finnish Ministry of Foreign Affairs, 2002

Rafi Segal and Eyal Weizman (ed.), *A Civilian Occupation: the Politics of Israeli Architecture*, Tel Aviv-Jaffa, New York, 2003

Simon Sheikh (ed.), *Oe Critical Readers in Visual Cultures #5: In the Place of the Public Sphere?*, Berlin, 2005

Thomas Sieverts, *Cities Without Cities: An Interpretation of the Zwischenstadt*, London, 2003

SKOR (ed.), *Mixed Farming: The Changing Agrarian Landscape*, Rotterdam, 2004

Stephanie Smith, *Ecologies: Mark Dion, Peter Fend, Dan Peterman*, Smart Musuem of Art, University of Chicago, 2001

Rebecca Solnit, *Wanderlust: A History of Walking*, London, 2004

Susan G. Solomon, *American Playgrounds: Revitalizing Community Space*, Hanover-London, 2005

*Temporary Territories: Works by Kerstin Bergendal* (Exhibition Catalogue), Copenhagen, Nikolaj, Copenhagen Contemporary Art Center, 2005

Thalia Theater Halle (ed.), *Hotel Neustadt* , Berlin, 2004

Alexander Tzonis and Liane Lefaivre, *Critical Regionalism*, 1958

UN-HABITAT (United Nations Centre for Human Settlements), *The State of the World's Cities Report 2001*, Nairobi, 2002

——, *An urbanizing world: Global report on human settlements*, Oxford, 1996

——, *The challenge of slums: Global report on human settlements*, London, 2003

UN-HABITAT Best Practice database www.bestpractices.org

John Urry, *Consuming Places*, London, 1995

Gavin Wade, *The Interruptors,* Birmingham, 2005

Lynne Warren Dan Peterman, Plastic Economies, Illinois 2004.

William H. Whyte, *The Social Life of Small Urban Spaces*, New York: Project for Public Spaces, 1980

www.worldchanging.com

Wolfgang Zinggl (ed.), *WochenKlausur: Sociopolitical Activism in Art*, Vienna, 2001

# ILLUSTRATION CREDITS

# INDEX